Single Card Strategies
for
Magic: The Gathering™

Jeff Franzmann, Philip Kramer,

and Beth Moursund

Wordware Publishing, Inc.

Library of Congress Cataloging-in-Publication Data

Franzmann, Jeff.
Single Card Strategies for Magic: The Gathering / Jeff Franzmann, Philip Kramer, and Beth Moursund.
p. cm.
Includes index.
ISBN 1-55622-489-3 (pbk.)
1. Magic: The Gathering (Game). I. Franzmann, Jeff.
II. Moursund, Beth. III. Title.
GV1469.62.M34K73 1996
793.93'2--dc20 96-447
CIP

1506 Capital Avenue
Plano, Texas 75074

Printed in the United States of America

ISBN 1-55622-489-3

10 9 8 7 6 5 4 3 2 1
9602

All inquiries for volume purchases of this book should be addressed to Wordware Publishing, Inc., at the above address. Telephone inquiries may be made by calling:

(214) 423-0090

Contents

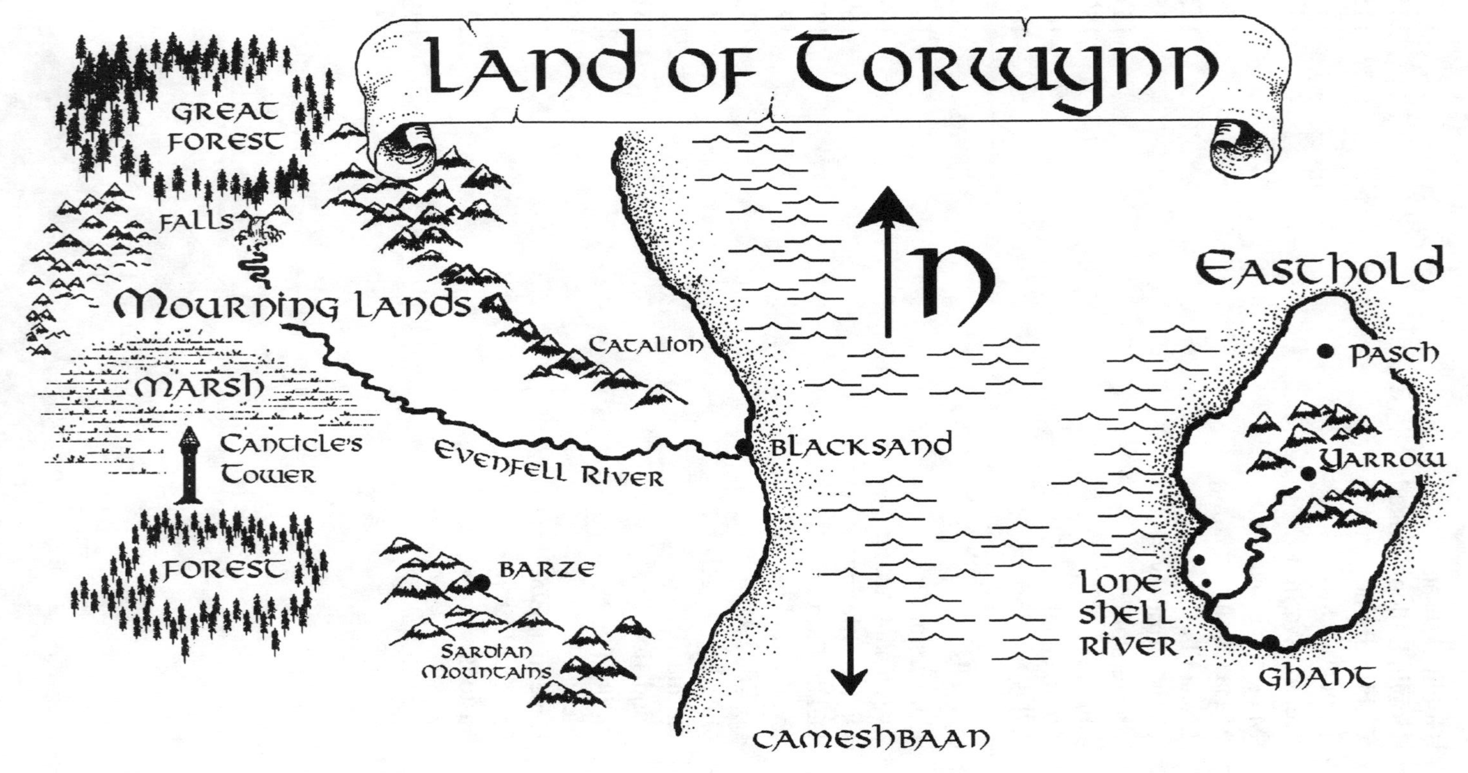
Land of Torwynn
Great Forest
Falls
Mourning Lands
Marsh
Canticle's Tower
Forest
Evenfell River
Catalion
Blacksand
Barze
Sardian Mountains
N
Cameshbaan
Easthold
Pasch
Yarrow
Lone Shell River
Ghant

Foreword

Books on games delight me.

My shelves are filled with books describing games and talking about strategies in games. Some of the books are regular references of mine. Some of the games analyzed, like Blackjack, I never was attracted to, and don't ever expect to be attracted to, but the process of strategic evaluation was fascinating, and so the book took on a value beyond the game. Books on game strategy add credibility to a game, and the gaming field as a whole.

Single Card Strategies grew out of a popular series of posts on the Internet. It is nice to have such a focused approach to the complicated subject of Magic™ strategy. In some ways it is a breakthrough book for Magic™, since to my knowledge it is the first book which is not ***generally*** on the game as a whole, but like books on chess openings, or bridge on slam bidding, this book concentrates on individual cards and their relations.

And the stories attached to each card are fun to read, also!

Richard Garfield

Acknowledgments

The authors would like to express their gratitude and appreciation to Richard Garfield and the other game designers, without whom we would have nothing to write about.

Dedications

To Erik, Ethan, Olee, Rick & Zippy (drinks are on me) for not being in the 98% category, other individuals I may have forgotten in my haste, and Andrew Eldritch for Lucretia, My Reflection.

—Jeff Franzmann

To Craig & Mike (for introducing me to M:TG), Lenore (for putting up with it), and the Dead General's Society (for being willing victims).

—Phil Kramer

To Dave "Snark" Howell, for giving me the chance.

—Beth 'Bethmo' Moursund

Artifacts

Armageddon Clock
(Antiquities, Revised, 4th Edition)

The smell of freshly turned earth filled the tunnel, evidence of the excavation that was taking place beneath the ruins of Ta Sin Razal. Long before the great war, the decadent city had fallen to ruin, burying with it secrets and relics that were best left beyond the reach of mortal hands. Now, gnarled hands wielding a pick disturbed centuries of long silence.

Card Name:	Armageddon Clock
Color:	Artifact
Spell Type:	Artifact
Casting Cost:	6 Colorless
P/T:	-

Add counter during upkeep. At the end of your upkeep, do 1 damage for each counter on Clock. Anyone may spend 4 during any upkeep to remove a counter.

The withered little creature rested his weight on the handle of the pick for a moment, wiping a wrinkled brow with his free hand. His leathery skin seemed stretched over his bones, and his sparse grey beard gave the appearance of great age. Yet when he began work once again, he wielded the pick with the enthusiasm of youth. It was not long before he was rewarded with a metallic clang. Brushing aside a layer of moist earth, the creature exposed a strange dial. Cackling wickedly, he turned to face the shadows behind him.

*"M'lord, I've found the **Armageddon Clock**"*

A magnificent and terrible device, the Clock costs 6 mana to summon forth. From that point onward, it accumulates a counter during each of your upkeeps. At the end of your upkeep, each player takes damage equal to the number of counters on the Clock. Any Mage may spend 4 mana to remove a counter during upkeep. A creation of the truly devious, of what use could such a machine possibly be?

Utilizing the Clock properly requires forethought and timing. It will not do to have this mechanism in play without the means to avoid its effects. The most obvious way of using the Armageddon Clock is in conjunction with the Circle of Protection: Artifacts. Simply pay mana to avoid the damage. Since the Clock will continue to accumulate counters, your opponent either takes damage or taps out mana to remove counters. A more limited method of preventing damage involves Reverse Polarity or even Reverse Damage. As the Clock ticks away, your opponent will quickly become convinced that you have gone mad, determined to destroy you both. Once 4 counters have accumulated on the Clock, simply cast Reverse Damage or Reverse Polarity. The resulting gain in life, combined with the loss suffered by your opponent, should provide you with a comfortable lead. If you're more offensively minded, and the damage from Armageddon Clock is proving dangerous, cast Titania's Song for a 6/6 creature. Or, if you prefer, use Xenic Poltergeist or Animate Artifact. . .note that while the Clock is tapped, counters cannot be removed.

Equally effective, though more blatant, is combining the Clock with life-giving magicks. Using spells such as Drain Life, Stream of Life or Soul Burn in conjunction with the Armageddon Clock can result in a life total that provides you with a cushion against the Clock. Less obvious but equally effective are the Martyrs of Korlis, especially if they have been enchanted with an Artifact Ward.

Part of the Clock's power, however, is psychological. The effect of watching life whittled away slowly will often cause an opponent to drain his or her pool of mana to remove counters from the device. All told, the Armageddon Clock can be a frightening addition to any Magi's arsenal.

Bandares stepped forward to examine the device, rubbing his pointed chin in thought. He extended a spidery arm to brush more earth from the surface of the device, and smiled malevolently.

"My friend, it's the end of the world as we know it."

The small creature nodded at Bandares, tugging at his beard.

"Won't that toss off a few folks right and proper. . . ."

Copper Tablet

(Alpha, Beta, Unlimited)

The port city of Blacksand is haven to the malcontents and miscreants of Torwynn, a ramshackle collection of refugees, traders and merchants from across the known world. Against the backdrop of seedy brothels, rotting homes and abandoned buildings, the marbled spires of the Temple of the Artificers seem oddly out of place.

Deep within the corridors of the Temple, an ancient device stirs to life. Mystic symbols of ancient power surround the pedestal upon which it resides, and flare to life as the eldritch stone responds to far off call. The surface of the pedestal shines with a dim, eerie, light, illuminating the ***Copper Tablet****.*

Card Name:	**Copper Tablet**
Color:	**Artifact**
Spell Type:	**Artifact**
Casting Cost:	**2 Colorless**
P/T:	-

All players take 1 damage during their upkeep as long as Copper Tablet is in play.

Few were the Magi who mastered the use of this device before it disappeared from the face of Torwynn. Costing only 2 mana, the toll this creation took was often considered too great. The power of the Tablet was such that it would cause 1 damage to each player during his or her upkeep. However, many methods have since been developed which allow the Tablet to be used to its full potential.

Obviously, as with the Armageddon Clock, numerous methods of preventing the damage should be available before using this device. As with the Clock, the Circle of Protection: Artifacts is the ideal choice. The Martyrs of Korlis are also an excellent alternative, since the one damage done by the Tablet will hardly be taxing on their abilities. The effects provided by the Conservator, Fountain of Youth or even the Samite Healer can all be used to dampen the effects of the Tablet on you, while causing your opponent problems.

Unlike the Clock, there are even more effective ways of avoiding the damage available. Tapping the Tablet by means of the Icy Manipulator, Phyrexian Gremlins or even the Elder Druid before or during your upkeep prevents the damage from ever taking place. After your upkeep has passed, use the Elder Druid, Twiddle, or some other effect to untap the Tablet.

On its own, the Tablet may not be an effective source of damage. However, combined with spells and artifacts like the Armageddon Clock, Cursed Land and the Ankh of Mishra, it can quickly contribute to the imminent destruction of an opponent. With the Martyrs of Korlis, the combination of Ankh, Clock and Tablet is truly frightening; while you are taking no damage, your opponent is withering at an incredible rate.

The Copper Tablet is a cheap and effective method of tying down an opponent, especially if you have the means to deal with the damage it is inflicting. A foe will often concentrate his or her efforts on destroying the Tablet, allowing you more freedom to act.

A line of monks filed past the room, hardly sparing a second glance in the direction of the pedestal. The ruins had been disturbed, or the Tablet would never have come to life, but there was little concern. Long before any of them had been brought forth into the world, the Tablet had done its duty. And it would continue to do so long after they were dust.

Meekstone

(Alpha, Beta, Unlimited, Revised, 4th Edition)

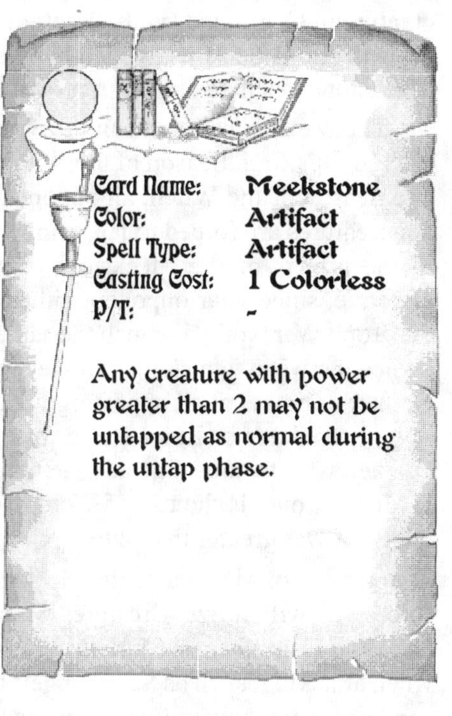

Usually, the sounds of the forest bring comfort and solace to the weary heart. Birds of all description sing, squirrels chatter amidst the boughs and branches of ancient oak, and the wind dances through the leaves. Not so in the woods that border the Mourning Lands. The oppressive sound of silence surrounds the ear.

Canticle brushed roots, moss, and grass from the surface of the oddly glowing stone, carefully removing it from the hollow of a decaying oak stump. Eyes narrowing, he passed the yellow hunk of rock to a shivering, furry form which appeared to be little more than legs, arms, and bulbous eyes.

"Bandares will come to fear this stone, little one, be careful not to drop it."

The gremlin gave a salute, promptly dropping the rock on his foot. A high-pitched squeal bounced off the trees as the Necromancer rolled his eyes.

"Such a simple task, and as always, it ends up being more difficult than need be. Such is the nature of the ***Meekstone****."*

The Meekstone is a highly sought-after prize, for it costs only 1 mana and prevents any creature with a power greater than 2 from untapping as normal during the untap phase. The possibilities of such a device are many and varied.

One of the most common uses of this particular artifact is in conjunction with what has been called "Horde" magic. Combined with a large number of low-power, low-cost creatures, the Meekstone can be the deciding factor. Not only is a Mage able to get out a large number of small creatures in a short period of time, but the Meekstone prevents the opponent from taking advantage of his or her larger creatures. Combined with creature enhancements such as Giant Growth and Blood Lust, which bypass the restrictions imposed by the Meekstone, such an army can prove itself time and again.

The Meekstone itself can prove deadly when used in conjunction with Siren's Call, Season of the Witch, or Total War. With Siren's Call and Season of the Witch, an opponent will watch helplessly as his or her creatures are forced to tap, removing them from consideration due to the effects of the Meekstone. Season of the Witch is far more effective, since your opponent either attacks or watches his creatures die. Total War works in much the same way, forcing a player to make a choice between attacking with everything or not attacking at all. Neither option is at all appealing with a Meekstone in play. Using the Icy Manipulator or Elder Druid to force opposing creatures to tap is another way to take full advantage of the Meekstone. A particular favorite of ours is the use of Word of Binding to force every creature with a power greater than 2 to tap.

Of course, when using the Meekstone, you have to consider which forces you will utilize. Creatures which can be pumped, such as Killer Bees and Hoar Shades, Murk Dwellers, and creatures which do not tap when attacking, such as Serra Angels and Zephyr Falcons, are all ideal candidates for a variety of reasons. The Labyrinth Minotaur is an excellent addition, as you can block those few creatures your opponent has available for use, making them useless every other turn. Even if you include creatures like the Scaled Wurm or Stone Spirit, there are ways around the Meekstone. Instill Energy, Jandor's Saddlebags and even (for the desperate) Paralyze all allow you to untap creatures which would otherwise fall under the effects of the Meekstone. While Chain Stasis can allow you to untap several creatures in a turn, it can be a costly effect.

Canticle shook his head as the gremlin hoisted the rock over its shoulder and proceeded to fall flat on its back. It was going to be a long trip back to the tower. Pulling on the edges of his silver-trimmed vest, he began the long walk home.

Millstone
(Antiquities, Revised, 4th Edition)

West of the Mourning Lands, the looming spires of the Sardian Mountains march across the horizon. Amidst the forested valleys and glacial lakes, far from areas which any sane man would consider civilized, a tower sits atop a rocky crag. On this night, a single light shines through an open window, indicating that the Lord of the Mountain is home. And for that, many across Torwynn are thankful.

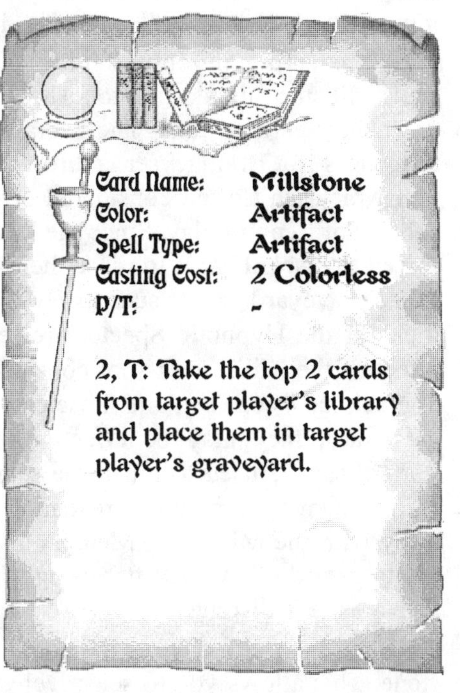

"How rude, not inviting me into their little contest. One would think that after so many entertaining conflicts, they'd have slightly more respect for my capabilities."

The Lord of the Mountain paced his chamber, tongues of fire licking from a head which appeared to be engulfed in flames. His red hair splayed out in all directions, contrasting horribly with his wildly mismatched robes. So anxious was his pacing that one of his furry loafers had fallen from his foot and was lying in the center of the room.

Finally, he stopped before the door next to his bed and flung it open in anger.

"All right, enough slacking. Faster I say. . . ."

The Lord glared at the three gremlins which were chained to a large gear assembly. Fuzzy hands grasped wooden handles as they walked in circles, operating what appeared to be some sort of arcane ***Millstone****.*

At a cost of 2 mana, the Millstone is a key component in many Denial decks. When 2 mana are paid, and the Millstone is tapped, the top two cards of the target player's library are placed in the graveyard. While the benefits of such an artifact are immediately obvious—the destruction of opposing resources—there are a variety of methods which can be used to increase the effectiveness of this destruction. Too many individuals simply try to run an opponent out of cards with multiple Millstones. While amusing, it is hardly effective.

For example, if you wish to speed up the destruction of a library, use a Millstone in addition to a Howling Mine, effectively chewing it down four cards a turn. The average library won't last past fifteen turns, less if a Braingeyser is thrown in for effect. Another combination which isn't often considered occurs when your opponent has a Library of Leng in play. Since the Library allows an opponent who is forced to discard cards to place them on top of the Library instead of in the graveyard, spells such as Hymn to Tourach and effects such as those of the Hypnotic Specter are severely curtailed. However, the effect of the Millstone is not considered a discard. Once a Hymn to Tourach has been cast, and those cards have been place on top of the graveyard, they may be effectively and conveniently Millstoned. Portent can be used to much the same effect. Simply place the two cards which appear most threatening on top of the library and grind away with the Millstone. Memory Lapse is another method you can use to get rid of spells. After using Memory Lapse to counter a spell, activate the Millstone.

Even more effective is the combination of Orcish Spy and Millstone. This allows you to selectively target an opponent's library for destruction. Simply forcing removal to the graveyard at random can be a chancy thing; at times, it may bring a card to the top of the library which you would rather have never seen surface. Millstoning two Mountains when the third card is a Shivan Dragon is not exactly a happy event.

Millstone can also be used to your benefit, on yourself. A classic reanimation strategy is to Millstone powerful creatures into your graveyard (using spells like Brainstorm, Diabolic Vision or Orcish Spy to discern their location), and reanimate them using Animate Dead or Dance of the Dead. If you have Lhurgoyf or the Wall of Tombstones, or other creatures which benefit from bloated graveyards, Millstone can be an effective method of supplying them with fuel.

The Lord of the Mountain nodded as the gremlins increased their pace, and he closed the door. It was so hard to get good help these days. He quickly turned his attention to the matter at hand. . .the grievous slight he had suffered at the hands of both Canticle and Bandares.

"Hrmph, imagine forgetting to include me in their little jaunt. Well, every good contest needs rules, and rules are always enforced by some sort of referee. . . ."

The Lord of the Mountain began rummaging around inside a large oaken chest, ignoring the fact that he had just set fire to his bedsheets.

"Now where in the name of all the hells above and below is that whistle? . . ."

Winter Orb

(Alpha, Beta, Unlimited, Revised, 4th Edition)

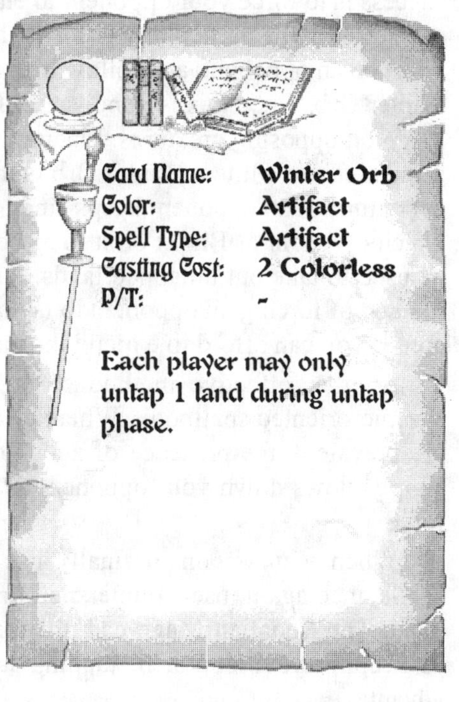

A rime of frost covered everything in sight, the only indication that something unnatural had taken place. The trees and flowers in the courtyard had blackened and died, unable to derive sustenance from the frozen earth. The guard appeared to be asleep at his post, using his pike as support. Only on closer inspection did one realize that he was dead, frozen in place.

Inside the castle, the arctic chill was even more noticeable. Light from the summer sun poured in through open windows, yet the film of ice remained intact. And within the High Chamberlain's laboratories, the mysterious object responsible for the disaster sat upon a table. How was the elderly chamberlain to know that the strange sphere recovered from the Deadlands was a ***Winter Orb****?*

A potent artifact costing a mere 2 mana, the Winter Orb prevents the untapping of more than 1 land during the untap phase. In the proper circumstances, this can be a crippling device.

Obviously, this device is best used when one is prepared to deal with low land resources. Making intensive use of non-land sources of mana in conjunction with the storage lands (Sand Silos, Bottomless Vaults and so forth) is the most effective method by far. Dark Rituals, Fyndhorn and Llanowar Elves, Birds of Paradise and Fellwar Stones are the most popular spells and creatures by far. Ley Druids can also be used to untap additional lands. Once you are prepared to accept the consequences, you can begin to make things difficult for your opponent.

Since the Winter Orb prevents the untapping of land, the key to success is to force your opponent to either tap land or suffer some sort of ill effect. One particularly cruel method of doing this is to cast Mana Short on an opponent, and follow it up immediately with the casting of Winter Orb. Once this is done, start placing Errant Minion and Mind Whip on opposing creatures. Placing Mind Whip and Seizures on the same creature while a Winter Orb is in play almost assures 5 damage every turn. If an opponent keeps land untapped during your turn, place Psychic Venom or Blight on it to discourage use. Stone Rain can also be used to take out untapped lands. Power Sink can also be used as a method of forcing an opponent to tap lands but should only be considered if you can afford to expend the mana yourself.

Another effective method of utilizing the Winter Orb is in a Weenie-oriented spellbook. Where creatures costing only 1 or 2 mana are prevalent, the presence of a Winter Orb is hardly detrimental. It simply slows down your opponent as you acquire a large and potent force.

When your opponent finally has enough land to begin casting spells once again, use Counterspell or Force Spike to keep the upper hand. The Vodalian Mage can also prove useful in these situations, as keeping your opponent tapping lands is almost always to your advantage.

The Winter Orb is also an excellent way to get by the effects of specialty lands such as the Maze of Ith or the Library of Alexandria. If these lands are used, they either remain tapped due to the Winter Orb, or they are untapped. . .and if they are untapped, it means that no land is available to provide mana.

One particularly cruel way of avoiding the effects of the Orb while forcing your opponent to deal with them is elegant and simple. During your opponent's turn, after his untap phase, tap the Winter Orb using the Phyrexian Gremlins. During your untap phase, you may freely untap your land, the Gremlins, and the Winter Orb. The Icy Manipulator and Relic Barrier are more widely used than the Gremlins, due to their nature as artifacts, and work just as effectively. In addition, the Manipulator can be used to tap lands that your opponent untaps, if you can afford the expense.

Obviously, the Winter Orb is a potent device. In the right circumstances, it can almost completely shut down an opposing spellbook while at the same time barely affecting your ability to counter spells.

Bandares clicked his tongue in annoyance as he moved the frozen body of the chamberlain aside. Flesh tore from his hands as he pulled them away from the corpse, and he cursed under his breath, frost forming on his upper lip.

"When you pay your help this well, you expect them to listen. Now I'm going to have to figure this one out myself, and I have far better things to do with my time."

Black Spells

Animate Dead

(Alpha, Beta, Unlimited, Revised, 4th Edition)

Twin moons hung over the Marsh, pale and wan, bathing the region in a ghostly luminescence. Trees were limned with the fey light, and the flicker of distant stars reflected eerily off stagnant pools. Against the backdrop of the night sky, the Tower stood amidst the reeds and fens, home to Canticle, Necromancer Emeritus of the Institute.

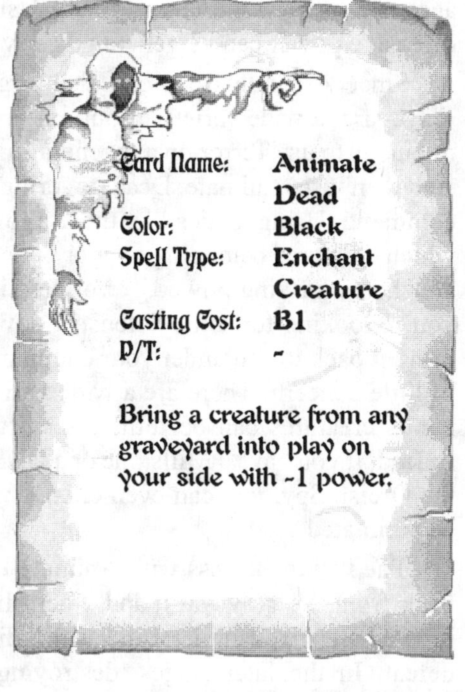

Thinning black hair brushed neatly back revealed a widow's peak and neatly trimmed sideburns. His green eyes concentrated on the task at hand, his lithe frame swathed in the black, silver-lined vest and dark trousers which were his hallmark. He stood over a brackish pool of algae and slime, sickly reeds poking forth from its surface, immersed in the ritual of spell casting. The coming contest dictated that he take the extreme measure of casting a spell to ***Animate Dead****.*

At a cost of 1 Black mana and 1 Colorless, this enchantment can be used on any creature which resides within a graveyard, yours or your foe's. The creature is brought into play on your side with a penalty of -1/0, weakened as it is from its encounter with death.

One of the most popular uses for this enchantment involves reviving creatures which never even entered play. As a result, creatures with significant power levels and a correspondingly high cost can be brought into play with minimal effort. For example, a Shivan Dragon which would normally cost 7 mana to bring into play can be called forth for only 2. Indeed, it is often advantageous to force the discard of your more powerful cards in the early stages of a duel, bringing them into play with Animate Dead. Using Mind Bomb, Jandor's Ring, or the Dwarven Armourer, you can toss creatures such as the Mahamoti Djinn, Serra Angel, and Seraph into the graveyard. The very next turn, they can be brought into play with Animate Dead, even if you have access to meager amounts of mana. Using this method, a great deal of offensive power can be generated early on in the duel.

Since Animate Dead can also target creatures in an opponent's graveyard, a wide variety of options are available. A favorite method of ours is to use Terror on a regenerating creature belonging to our foe, and then use Animate Dead to bring it back into play under our command. Using tactics like these allow you to selectively determine which creatures belonging to your opponent you wish to utilize. If you are short on flying power, Terror an Air Elemental and Animate it. If you're looking for some defensive power, Drain Life a wall and then bring it back to life under your command, where the reduced power is of little concern. There are a wide variety of ways in which an opponent's creatures can be turned against him using this enchantment. Indeed, if you have a Millstone or a Disrupting Scepter, combined with the Orcish Spy, you can even choose which creatures will ultimately be Animated.

The key to success with Animate Dead is knowing what to bring back from the graveyard, and when. In the early stages of a duel, a revived Sengir Vampire can be the difference between victory and defeat. In the later stages, destroying an opponent's Serra Angel, bringing it back onto your side, can alter the balance of power.

Dealing with Animate Dead is somewhat more problematic. Obviously, anything which removes creatures from the graveyard will be to your benefit if you want to avoid having it Animated. Night Soil, Eater of the Dead, and Tormod's Crypt are a few of the obvious ones. Using the Cyclopean Mummies in lieu of other creatures is a less obvious, though effective, way of reducing the risk as well. A simple Disenchant or Tranquility will terminate the problem in any event.

The waters churned, and a sickly, mottled hand broke through the film of algae. Grasping a nearby root, the newly reborn creature pulled itself from the marsh which had been its grave for so long, brine dripping from the remnants of its jaw, eyeless sockets gazing at the still night sky.

Canticle cursed the name of Bandares, that it forced him to such lengths. He straightened his vest, and strengthened his resolve. It mattered little. . .if he failed, it would not be long before all Torwynn came to regret it.

Ashes to Ashes

(The Dark, 4th Edition)

Card Name: Ashes to Ashes
Color: Black
Spell Type: Sorcery
Casting Cost: BB1
P/T: -

Remove two non-artifact creatures from the game and lose 5 life.

Three cloaked figures made their way down the darkened streets of Blacksand, a miasma following in their wake. None dared confront them, so great was the aura of fear which surrounded them. The lead figure chanted slowly, haltingly, in a tongue which seemed familiar, yet ancient beyond imagining. The second held a bell; the heavy tones which it produced filled the air.

They stopped before the hostel and waited. They could afford patience, for they had all the time in the world. Their master was ready, having defeated the greatest threat he had ever known. . .he could wait for his minions to complete their task.

It wasn't long at all before two men left the hostel, fear etched on their faces, bodies shivering involuntarily at the sight of the three robed figures. Unshaven and unwashed, they had been fleeing their fate for weeks. Only now it had caught up to them.

"Sanctus Ashnodi, in nominae Bandares . . . ***Ashes to Ashes.*** *"*

A Sorcery of dread power, this spell costs 2 Black mana and 1 Colorless, making it slightly more expensive than Terror. Its effects, however, are far worse, for it vaporizes 2 non-artifact creatures, removing them from the game without hope of regeneration or retrieval. The cost is high, however, for it deals 5 points of damage to the caster.

The utility of this spell is often overlooked due to the high cost involved in its casting. While 5 damage is not insignificant, one must consider the alternatives. In an attack situation, where your opponent has several powerful blockers, Ashes to Ashes may open up enough of a gap to allow you to inflict a large amount of damage to your foe. A stalemate can quickly be brought to an end when an equal number of creatures are facing off against each other as well, simply by knocking out the two most powerful creatures available to your opponent. In cases like this, the 5 damage you receive may be paltry compared to what you can inflict on your opponent.

Of course, you aren't required to take the damage either. There is nothing preventing you from activating a Circle of Protection: Black or using a Reverse Damage to counter the damaging effects of Ashes to Ashes. Indeed, in a White/Black spellbook, Ashes to Ashes can be the ideal replacement for Terror. Reverse Damage is the most poignant way of dealing with the effect of the spell . . . not only are you dealing with two of your opponent's creatures with one spell, you're gaining life in the process as well.

Another thing which makes Ashes to Ashes appealing is the fact that it utterly removes the creatures in question from existence. Raise Dead, Regrowth, Death Ward—nothing will return them from the void. Obviously, this makes the spell extremely appealing to those who face Magi who delight in reanimation tactics. As well, unlike Terror, Ashes to Ashes can target Black creatures, making it slightly more utilitarian than Terror.

When using Ashes to Ashes, always keep in mind that your own life must be carefully measured against that of your opponent. One should never utilize the spell unless one can be assured of ending the turn in the lead in terms of life points. While risk garners reward, excessive risk is simply foolish. Used in conjunction with Drain Life, Stream of Life, Life Chisel and so forth, it can be an excellent replacement for Terror.

When one has few life-providing spells, however, it can be more trouble than it's worth.

The two men were surrounded by an unholy light and opened their mouths as if to scream; there was no sound, however. In moments, nothing remained save a film of dust in the air which quickly settled to the ground and dispersed on the light breeze.

The three robed figures turned their backs on the hostel, and made their way down the street. Their master would be pleased.

Cursed Land

(Alpha, Beta, Unlimited, Revised, 4th Edition)

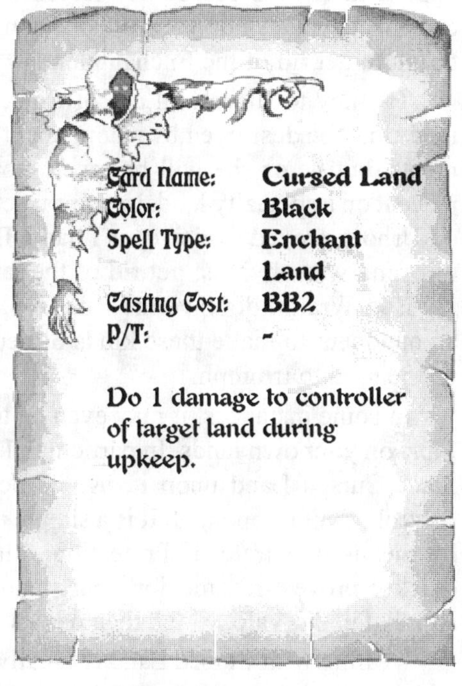

The Lord of the Mountain winced as his foot touched the blasted soil. Shaking his head, he began dictating notes to the small goblin which followed close behind him. A pair of wire frame glasses was perched on the goblin's nose, and he held a ridiculously large feather quill in his free hand. The other was taken up by his writing tablet. The Lord of the Mountain spoke in clear, measured tones.

"It doesn't take much imagination to realize that the abomination responsible for this scene is Canticle. Or Bandares. Assign them each a penalty, just to make sure. Now let's see. . .the grass is twisted and black, reeking of decay, the ground a carpet of ash. It's safe to assume that this is now ***Cursed Land****."*

Of the many powers available to the Necromancer, Cursed Land is perhaps the most insidious. At a cost of 2 Black mana and 2 Colorless, this enchantment can be placed on any land. From that point onward, during the upkeep of the target land's controller, Cursed Land does 1 damage to him or her.

Cursed Land often provides the most benefit when brought into play as early as possible. The 1 damage every turn can offset many beneficial enchantments, spells and artifacts. The effects of such artifacts as the Ivory Cup, Wooden Sphere and Throne of Bone, enchantments such as Lifetap, and the benefits provided by the Samite Healer can all be counteracted by an active Cursed Land. Indeed, if your opponent lacks the ability to heal or prevent damage, Cursed Land can be a potent offensive weapon in and of itself.

Bringing out Cursed Land early isn't difficult, despite the high casting cost. By means of a Dark Ritual, it can be in play as early as the second turn, and multiple Cursed Lands can quickly drain an opponent. In this respect, it serves a dual purpose. Not only is it causing damage, but your opponent may tie up time and resources trying to get rid of the Enchantment.

The key to successful use of Cursed Land is in placement: basic lands may be destroyed by an opponent to get rid of negative enchantments, but he or she will be much more loathe to do so should you place it on a specialty land. In one particular duel, placing Cursed Land on Urborg proved decisive, as I had a Bog Wraith in my employ. The dilemma was obvious: get rid of the land and lose the ability to stop my Bog Wraith, or leave the land in place and take damage. Forcing an opponent to make these kinds of decisions is one of the first steps on the road to triumph.

In some instances, it may even be to your benefit to place Cursed Land on your own lands. In particular, I am referring to Rainbow Vale. Place Cursed Land upon it, use its power, and it will revert to the control of your opponent. It is a simple matter to avoid the return favor by means of Circle of Protection: Black. Such a combination can quickly prove tiresome for your opponent; to activate your Circle, simply tap the Vale, which then passes on to your opponent.

Dealing with Cursed Land is usually a matter of taking out the land which it enchants. While anything which takes out an Enchantment will work, land protection spells like Equinox are useless. Combined with Psychic Venom, Cursed Land can cause a great deal of problems. The best method remains a Circle of Protection, as it allows you to continue using the land which is Cursed.

The Lord of the Mountain took a step back as a tremendous explosion sounded from the woods ahead of him. Trees burst into flames, and burning tinder fell in a shower around him. A small, dark sphere in the sky grew larger and larger, hurtling towards him with astonishing speed. He blinked and at the last moment leapt aside as the furry missile impacted at the point where he had only recently been standing. The gremlin shook its head, and steadied itself with its hands. Unfortunately, the tainted ground burned its unholy flesh, and the beast howled in pain. It leapt into the air, and began dancing around, hopping from foot to foot as the land scorched its feet.

The Lord of the Mountain pointed in the direction of the woods and motioned for his goblin assistant.

"I believe it's this way. . . ."

Cyclopean Mummy

(Legends, 4th Edition)

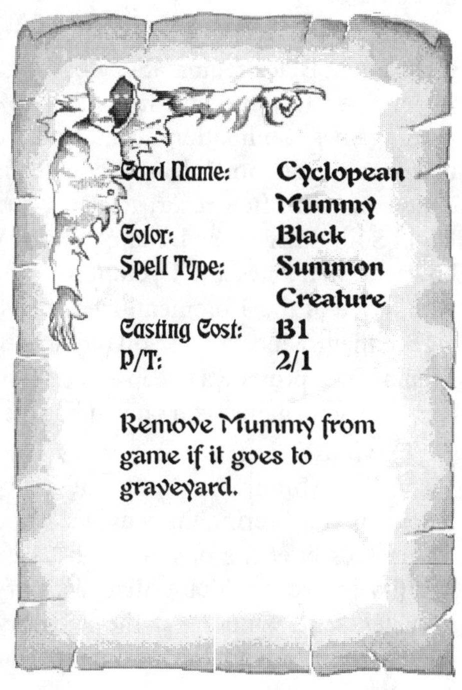

Hassan gingerly brushed aside cobweb strands which had been accumulating for centuries, using his scimitars to force a path through the sand-choked corridor. The blades glinted with an inner light, the only illumination available to him in this deserted tomb. The sound of mail bouncing against oiled riding leathers was startlingly clear, and echoed alarmingly with his every step.

The people of the village lived in a state of near constant terror, and as a result had called upon the services of the Ashashid. And the Ashashid had called upon

Hassan. It wasn't long before he had determined the cause of the disturbance. Somehow, someone had awakened a ***Cyclopean Mummy****.*

One of the most misunderstood and underutilized creatures, the Cyclopean Mummy receives a great deal of abuse. At a cost of 1 Black and 1 Colorless, you summon a 2/1 creature which is removed from the game upon reaching the graveyard. While many have argued that this renders the beast useless, there are some who would argue otherwise.

At its cost, the Cyclopean Mummy is one of the more efficiently powered creatures available to Black and can be a key component in the Black version of a Weenie Horde strategy. Combined with the Erg Raiders, Hasran Ogress, Vampire Bats and Drudge Skeletons, the basis for an effective army can be formed. Using the Ogress on defense, the Drudge Skeletons and Mummies can attack at will. Speed is the obvious advantage. A first turn Dark Ritual can summon a Cyclopean Mummy in addition to a Vampire Bat on the first turn, providing you with a significant opening advantage with a 2/1 ground attacker and a pumpable flyer. Few other Black creatures boast this kind of power-to-mana ratio.

One of the overlooked advantages to the Cyclopean Mummy is its inclusion in Black reanimation decks, and for obvious reasons. One has to consider, however, those spells and artifacts which are most often used against reanimation decks, and the effectiveness of the Mummy becomes a little more clear. When dealing with a reanimation deck, an opponent will often resort to using such spells and enchantments as Night Soil, Eater of the Dead, Spoils of War, and Spoils of Evil. Notice, however, that since the Cyclopean Mummy doesn't stay in the graveyard, none of the aforementioned spells and creatures can take advantage of them. Since Night Soil requires two creatures in a graveyard, the Mummy can provide a cheap and effective blocker. You have no fear of it being used against you once it has died.

Obviously, the Mummy has its drawbacks. Though immune to Terror, the Mummy is pretty much a one-shot creature. Once killed, there is no recovering the remains. Though few Necromancers trouble themselves over the demise of a */1 creature, they can actually be a liability in decks which utilize Wall of Tombstones or Frankenstein's Monster. When including the Mummy in a spellbook, take care to emphasize its advantages and remove any liabilities you may suffer as a result.

Hassan stepped into the open chamber, scimitars crossed before him. Though he had been expecting an attack, he was less than prepared for what happened next. Common belief is that the Mummy is a lumbering, careless beast, easily dispatched and sent to the Underworld. What leapt from the sarcophagus was far from lumbering, descending on the Ashashid with a fury born of a thousand lifetimes of awareness. Tendons and muscles taut with eldritch energies, its hands were almost at Hassan's throat before he was able to dispatch the creature.

Hassan glanced around the chamber before returning to the tunnel, making sure that there were no more beasts hidden in the shadows. The wakening of the Mummy could mean only one thing. The contest he had so long feared had begun.

Drain Life

(Alpha, Beta, Unlimited, Revised, 4th Edition)

Bandares pulled his dirty blond hair back and tied it with a red silk cord, whistling a tuneless song to himself all the while. A chill breeze wafted in through the open window, ruffling the sheets on the bed. He didn't seem to mind, however, and simply returned to what he was doing. His deerskin vest fit as well as it ever did, and he smiled a bit as he fiddled with the buttons. Never underestimate the importance of a first impression. Turning to the bed, he clapped his hands together.

"Well, I'd love to get to know you better, but I'm a little behind schedule. So if you don't mind. . . ."

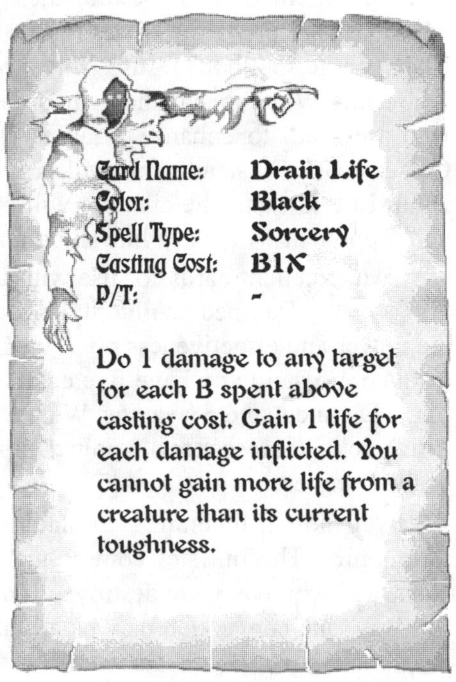

Bandares stepped up to the bound innkeeper, and placed a hand on the tubby man's forehead. In a growling chant, he uttered the ritual which would allow him to ***Drain Life****.*

At a cost of 1 Black mana and 1 Colorless, this Sorcery is one of the most effective available to the Necromancer. Once cast, each Black mana spent does one damage to a target creature or player, and for each damage dealt, provides the caster with 1 life. While you cannot drain more life than a target possesses, it is a potent spell indeed, especially when used under ideal circumstances.

Obviously, the most common use for this spell is against opposing creatures. Not only will you be taking out powerful defenders such as the Serra Angel and the Air Elemental, but in the process you will be adding to your life total. In dire situations, you may even consider using Drain Life against your own creatures, in order to increase your life total. While this obviously requires sufficient amounts of mana in your pool, this will hardly be a problem for a well-constructed deck.

Less obvious, but no less effective, are methods for increasing the lethality of Drain Life, and as a result, increasing the life it provides you. One method is to use toughness enhancing spells on creatures which you are preparing to destroy. A favorite method of mine is in a Black/White spellbook. . .use Holy Armor on a target creature, pump it up using White mana, and then Drain Life it using Black. For those who are loath to enhance a target creature in such a manner, use Creature Bond instead. This will provide three benefits to you when Drain Life is cast. The creature will be dead, you will gain life, and your opponent will lose a like amount as well. Chillingly effective.

Two excellent cards for use with Drain Life are Dark Ritual and Songs of the Damned. With only one swamp, you can vastly increase the power and effectiveness of Drain Life with these spells. Consider a situation where you have five creatures in your graveyard, a Songs of the Damned, and 5 swamps. What would have been a 3-point Drain Life quickly increases to a 7-point Drain Life, simply by casting Songs of the Damned.

Even more frightening is the addition of Initiates of the Ebon Hand to this mix. The Initiates convert mana into Black on a one-for-one basis, and while they are destroyed if more than 3 mana are converted this way, one conversion may be all that's necessary. Consider Channel, for example. If you Channel 19 life through the Initiates, and then power a Drain Life with that 19 Black mana, you deal that much damage to your opponent and receive that much life in return. The net loss of life to you is zero. Before the Initiates are buried at the end of the turn, have them attack, dealing that last point of damage. Chilling and effective.

Another grisly combination is Drain Life and Reverse Damage. Use Drain Life on yourself, and then proceed to cast Reverse Damage. This in effect provides you with double the life you would normally receive. Drain Life yourself for 10 points, you gain 10 life back; however, when Reverse Damage is cast, it reduces the damage dealt by Drain Life to 0 and adds it to your total, for a net gain of 20 life.

And if all else fails, you can always Fork it.

Bandares smiled as the life drained from the innkeeper, infusing his body with power and energy for the coming battle. He kept the man clinging to the edges of life. . .there was no need to draw suspicion on his person as of yet. A sleeping innkeeper would elicit little comment; a dead one would be fodder for the town crier.

Tightening his belt and placing his antler handled knife in its sheath, Bandares opened the door. Whistling the same tuneless song, he left the building and wandered out into the streets of Blacksand.

El-Hajjaj

(Arabian Nights, Revised, 4th Edition)

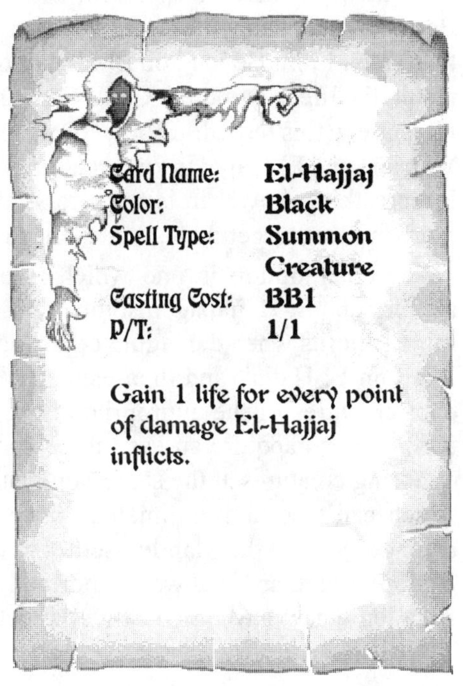

Canticle walked towards the pier, certain that he was too late. Indeed, he was, for the Devil Dancer was nowhere to be seen, having set sail earlier in the evening.

A lean man, a well-kept beard accenting his features and lending a calm demeanor on his face, walked from the crowded docks towards the

Necromancer. He wore a black turban and loose-fitting robes of similar color, marking him as a Tarkaan from the southern lands. Only the nobles or the Ashashid would dare wear black. Canticle narrowed his eyes as the man approached.

"Fair day, noble stranger. . . ."

Canticle hmphed. Since the contest had begun, his days had been anything but fair. Even the weather cooperated with his mood. . .today, the sky was blanketed by storm clouds.

"Allow me to introduce myself. . .I am the Tarkaan ***El-Hajjaj****."*

At a cost of 2 Black mana and 1 Colorless, the 1/1 El-Hajjaj is a potent investment indeed. For every point of damage inflicted by El-Hajjaj, his controller receives 1 life. While this life gain is limited to the toughness of the creature or the life of your opponent, it can still be considerable.

One of the first concerns when utilizing El-Hajjaj is how to improve the benefits provided by his abilities. While sending him through unblocked with the assistance of Tawnos' Wand or the Dwarven Warriors is always advisable, 1 point of damage for 1 life is simply not enough to justify the cost. Fortunately, there are a variety of methods available to increase the effectiveness of El-Hajjaj.

One of the favored spells for use with this creature is Howl From Beyond. After using the Dwarven Warriors to render him unblockable, toss Howl From Beyond on El-Hajjaj to increase the damage, and as a result, the life is garnered. Giant Growth and Blood Lust can be just as effective in this regard. Another option for use along with the Dwarven Warriors and El-Hajjaj is Firebreathing. The advantage of Instants over Firebreathing, however, is surprise. An enchanted creature is always a more inviting target than an unenchanted one.

Another option is one which is often overlooked. While most people send El-Hajjaj against the opposing Mage, he still provides the same benefits when damaging opposing creatures. Consider placing a Ward on El-Hajjaj, and then using the Nettling Imp or Norrit to call over creatures of the appropriate color. With an Unholy Strength or two, you can acquire an easy three or five lives a turn, and take out opposing creatures at the same time. Farrel's Mantle is another option which can't be underestimated; since it is the creature dealing the damage, and not the Mantle itself, you can destroy a creature and gain 2 more life than you would normally from El-Hajjaj. Consider a situation where a Mantled El-Hajjaj gets through and deals 1 damage to an opponent. Instead, you could have it deal 3 damage to a Hurloon Minotaur, killing it and gaining 3 life in the process.

Of course, El-Hajjaj does have drawbacks, the most obvious being its fragile nature. While this makes him highly susceptible to damage, the very things which protect him from damage also make him more of a threat. Unholy Strength, Holy Strength, and so on all increase power and toughness, which also increases the survivability and effectiveness of the card. The simplest way to shut down El-Hajjaj is through the use of a Circle of Protection: Black. Allowing him through and nullifying the damage means that no life is lost, your opponent gains no life, and you're saved the trouble of wasting an anti-creature spell on him.

Canticle nodded warily to the Tarkaan, unsure of what to make of his presence.

"What business do you have with me, Tarkaan?"

El-Hajjaj smiled, an unsettling sight.

"I've need of you, Necromancer, and you have need of me. I'm certain you'll find the name Bandares familiar to you, and I'm certain you'll be more than interested in an agreement which would see him. . .incapacitated."

Canticle smiled, and motioned towards one of the many taverns near the pier.

"My friend, we have much to discuss."

Evil Presence

(Alpha, Beta, Unlimited, Revised, 4th Edition)

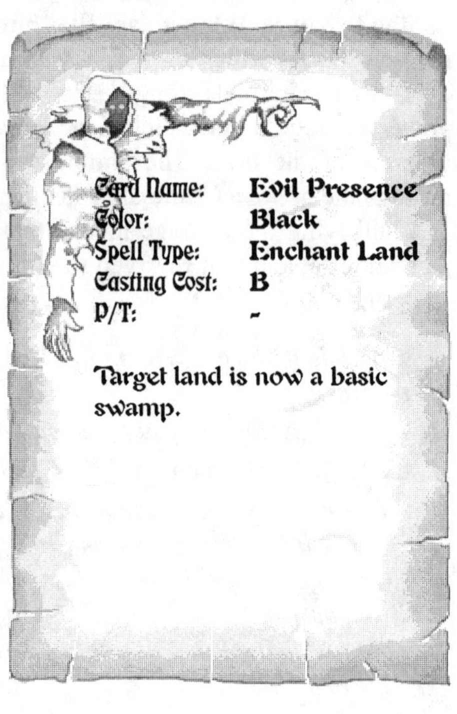

The ground sucked at their feet, pulling them into its embrace, clinging to their boots, refusing to surrender its hold. Gnats, flies, and insects of all description flocked around exposed flesh, stinging, biting, or simply hovering. The tang of decay was heavy in the air, and still they pressed on, returning to the tower.

Canticle knew he couldn't defeat Bandares in a race. There simply wasn't enough time. There were other ways of achieving victory, though, methods and rituals archaic beyond understanding. And so they were returning to the Mourning Lands, and his tower. Something was wrong however. . .even before they had completed the journey through the woods, the air took on an oppressive weight, the land a melancholy loathing. Everything seems tainted by an ***Evil Presence****.*

An enchantment costing only 1 Black mana, this spell allows the caster to turn any one land into a basic swamp. Since changeling magicks are usually the province of Blue, the inclusion of Evil Presence into a Black Spellbook can provide numerous benefits.

First and foremost, when dueling against Magi who do not utilize Black magic, Evil Presence can be used to infect their land, turning it into a swampy morass. This not only denies use of that land to your opponent for specific colored mana he or she may need, but allows you to utilize Swampwalking creatures such as the Lost Soul and Moor Fiend with abandon. This tactic is most effective when used against specialty lands. Libraries of Alexandria can be flooded with tepid waters, the City of Brass can sink beneath the bog, and the Elephant's Graveyard can be rendered useless.

Upkeep denial is another way in which Evil Presence can be effectively utilized, especially when spells with a cumulative upkeep are in play. If an opponent is using Drought or the Force of Nature, cast Evil Presence on one of the Plains or Forests which could be used to pay upkeep. This not only limits the options your opponent may have, but if he or she has been carefully husbanding resources, it may force him or her to abandon upkeep payments entirely. While this method almost requires that your opponent has the bare minimum of lands necessary for upkeep payment, it can be deadly when combined with the effects of Stone Rain or Blight.

Indeed, it is when used with land destruction that Evil Presence truly shines. A Blue/Red/Black Land Destruction tome, replete with Stone Rain, Blight, Phantasmal Terrain and Acid Rain can quickly render opposing lands useless. Evil Presence can turn what remains into a playground for Lost Souls and Bog Wraiths.

While Evil Presence can be a valued addition to your spellbook, always keep its limitations in mind. As an enchantment it is highly susceptible to a wide variety of spells, and since it enchants land, is open to the perils of Land Destruction as well. Using it on your own lands to provide additional Black mana, or to recover lands transformed by other spells, is always an option as well. The wide variety of uses available with Evil Presence make it well worth the investment.

Brushing aside strands of hanging moss, Canticle and his companion left the choking confines of the wood and looked out over the Mourning Lands. There still were the lonely stands of reeds, the low hillocks, the skeletal trees reaching into the starless night. Against the sky, there still stood the tower.

And over it all hung a hazy red cloud of ash and embers, boiling forth from the mountains in the far distance. Canticle sighed as he made his way towards the tower. . .the very land itself was beginning to heave in torment. Soon, the Beast would awaken.

Greed

(Legends, 4th Edition)

Card Name: **Greed**
Color: **Black**
Spell Type: **Enchantment**
Casting Cost: **B3**
P/T: **-**

B: Draw an extra card and sacrifice 2 life.

Ariana sat in a high-backed chair, wrapped in a quilted shawl which protected her frail form from the chill, damp air of the marsh. Her mousy brown hair was tied back with a length of cord, emphasizing her sallow features, and when she spoke, it was in a hacking whisper which made it hard for people to understand what she was saying. Canticle sat across from her, in rapt fascination. He had always respected her abilities, admired her as a person, but the tale she was weaving was unlike any he had heard before.

"When you were lost to us, for that time, the Master and his minions fell upon the East. The legions of Barze clashed with them along the banks of the Evenfell, and further as well. Katalion fell, in time. Blacksand grew more fetid and the bonds weakened. . . ."

Canticle shook his head, and his tanned companion stroked his beard in thought.

"The Beast feeds on ***Greed****."*

A potent enchantment indeed, Greed costs 1 Black mana and 3 Colorless. When activated, at a cost of 1 Black mana and two life points, you draw a card.

The applications of such a spell may not be immediately obvious, especially considering the costs involved. However, considering the numerous benefits inherit in Greed, they are well worth the price. Since the activation cost does not involve tapping, it can be used as many times as you wish during the course of a turn. In addition, there is nothing preventing you from using it during your opponent's turn as well. With this in mind, let us examine how to most effectively utilize Greed.

When used in combination with the Ivory Tower, Greed can more than pay for itself. If you have five or six cards in hand and an Ivory Tower in play, Greed allows you the luxury of drawing an extra card every turn, without worrying about an excessive loss of life. The Ivory Tower will be replenishing whatever you lose. In effect, this allows you access to more of your resources in a turn than you would usually be privy to. Combined with library searching methods such as Brainstorm, Orcish Spy, Visions, or what have you, Greed can even allow you to pick the card you want when you need it.

Against other cards, Greed can prove to be beneficial as well. If an opponent is using Zur's Weirding, Greed can force a situation where he or she either allows you to draw a card or gives up life that he or she can ill afford to lose. When facing down multiple Racks, Greed can provide you with that one extra card when you need it, for a one-time life point cost. In addition to these benefits, it can also allow you to replenish your hand after falling victim to card denial strategies. While the life point cost may prove troublesome, using Drain Life and Ivory Tower along with it can alleviate most of the damage.

Obviously, one has to measure cost versus gain. Greed allows you the advantage of drawing more resources at a cost of life. Early in the duel, this can be highly advantageous, allowing you to get an edge on your opponent. Later, when things are closer and changes occur more rapidly, it can prove disastrous. Experience has shown that using Greed earlier in the duel is to best advantage. Bringing it into play with Dark Ritual or using it multiple times in one turn is recommended over using it repeatedly over the course of a duel.

Canticle nodded, tapping his fingers against the worn surface of the table.

"And so it has awakened, in time for the contest. How wonderfully predictable of it. That creature has such a nose for the dramatic."

The Necromancer rose in disgust, and wandered over to a bookshelf, absently running a finger over dusty tomes and long-forgotten librams.

"All we need now is for that pompous Lord of the Mountain to stick his nose in things, and we'll have the makings of a real disaster."

Hypnotic Specter
(Alpha, Beta, Unlimited, Revised, 4th Edition)

"Pompous, am I? Stumbling around amidst the vapors of that Marsh has given him delusions of grandeur."

The Lord of the Mountain paced in a tight circle, flames above his head flickering as if they could sense his tension. His goblin scribe was seated a good distance away from the conflagration which surrounded his master, diligently scribbling notes.

"I dare say that he should be fined heavily for insulting an official. Perhaps a spell or two. . . ."

Tapping his chin in thought, the Lord of the Mountain snapped his fingers in inspiration.

"I have it! Oh Montgomery. . . ."

A filmy mist began to coalesce in the air before the Lord, slowly shaping itself into a vaguely humanoid form, encased in archaic armour. To the learned, it was immediately obvious that the Lord of the Mountain had enlisted the services of a ***Hypnotic Specter****.*

A Flying 2/2 creature, with a cost of 2 Black mana and 1 Colorless, the Hypnotic Specter is a potent weapon in the Necromancers arsenal. If the Specter deals damage to an opponent, he or she is also forced to discard a card at random.

One of the keys to successful use of the Specter is to bring it out early, easy enough if a Dark Ritual is on hand. On the first turn, the Specter can be out and about, ready to wreak havoc on an unsuspecting foe. This is immediately beneficial; not only will you be dealing damage early in the duel, but you will also be denying resources to your opponent at a stage when he or she needs them most. Combined with a second turn Hymn to Tourach, or used after a Mind Twist has emptied an opponent's hand of cards, the Specter can be a potent component in denial strategy.

The Specter can be made even more frightening through the use of Tawnos's Wand or the Dwarven Warriors. An unblockable Specter is something which no opponent will be willing to put up with for long, as it can quickly turn the tables in a duel. If the means to make your Specter unblockable are unavailable, use Unholy Strength, Unstable Mutation, or similar magicks to increase its effectiveness. There is nothing worse than a Hypnotic Specter which has Unstable Mutation placed on it the second turn of play. The drawbacks to Unstable Mutation are small, because by the time it is in its death throes, your opponent has probably placed an effective flying blocker into play. And in the meantime, you have had the benefit of a 5/5 creature that causes your opponent to discard a card.

Using the Rack, Disrupting Scepter, Hymn to Tourach, Mind Twist and similar such magicks in combination with the Hypnotic Specter makes for an incredibly annoying yet effective denial strategy. An opponent with no cards can hardly be considered a threat, after all.

When facing a Hypnotic Specter, a variety of methods exist to stave off the damage and discard. Since damage must be dealt in order for the discard to take place, the most effective defense is a high-powered flying blocker, or a Circle of Protection: Black. The Staff of Zegon could be used to render the Hypnotic an 0/2 creature, and Weakness can serve the same purpose. While deadly, the Specter is not invincible.

The Lord of the Mountain watched the Hypnotic Specter drift off towards the Mourning Lands with a self-satisfied smirk.

"I would love to see the look on his face when that thing drifts in through his bedroom window. Pompous indeed. I can't believe he's still on about the menace of the Beast. Fictive work of an overactive imagination I say, nothing more."

Junun Efreet
(Arabian Nights, 4th Edition)

Waves lapped against the sand, a gentle sound which filled the desert air with a calm and serenity unknown in lands beyond these shores. Hassan stood on the beach, allowing the waters to wash over his riding boots, his arms spread wide after a ritual of summoning.

A whisper filled the air, over the sound of the surf, and a light winked on the horizon. Soon, a blazing form appeared in the skies over the beach, brilliant orange fires limning a glistening, lavender body. Rings dangled from elven ears, and Hassan looked up at the ***Junun Efreet****.*

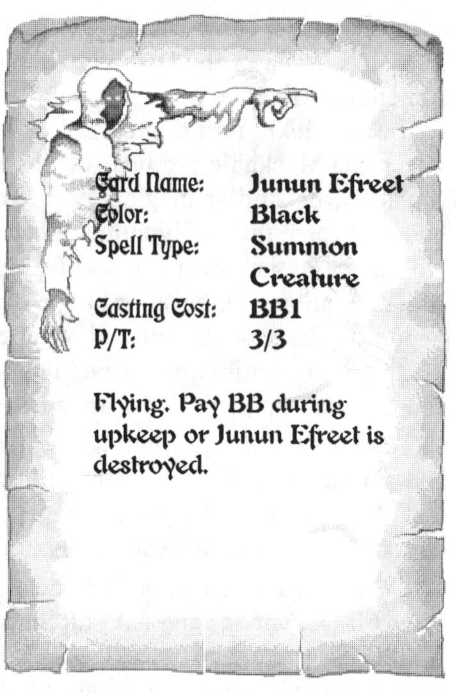

At a cost of 2 Black mana and 1 Colorless, this 3/3 flyer is one of the cheaper creatures available to the practitioner of Black. It is not without cost, however. During your upkeep, 2 Black mana must be paid or the Efreet is buried.

Due to its nature, it is usually more than just a little unwise to summon the Efreet on the first turn with a Dark Ritual. However, given its cost, its power and toughness, and the fact that it is a flying creature, the upkeep can be an easy thing to overlook when it is brought out on the second turn. A variety of methods exist to take advantage of the Junun Efreet's powers without being limited by its disadvantages, and this is what will be discussed below.

The ideal situation is to bring out Initiates of the Ebon Hand on the first turn, and on the second turn bring out a Sol Ring. With all of this in play on the second turn, summon forth the Junun Efreet, using the Initiates and the Sol Ring to pay upkeep on the Efreet from that point on. This allows you to use Dark Rituals for other purposes, while still taking advantage of the cheap cost of the Efreet. If Sol Rings are not available, other sources of fast mana can be substituted, although this may delay the arrival of the Efreet by a turn. If you use Dark Ritual on the second turn, the only real delay will be in the further casting of spells. In any event, by the time the Efreet hits the table, it will probably be the strongest flyer out. Once it ceases to serve a useful purpose, it can be sacrificed as a blocker, or you can simply refuse to pay the upkeep. Ideally, before refusing to pay the upkeep, you sacrifice it to the Life Chisel, or make use of it as fodder for the Fallen Angel.

In most instances, you'll want to use the Junun Efreet as a quick shock troop, while you build up resources for the bigger guns. Use the Junun until you can bring out a Fallen Angel, then sacrifice the Junun to the Angel and attack with a 5/4 flyer. Alternately, you may wish to utilize the Junun on defense as an expendable blocker once a deadlier flyer is in the air. In any event, the Junun can provide Black with an effective early flyer, at less cost than one may think.

The Efreet descended, hovering above the waves, acknowledging Hassan with a dip if his horned head. The Ashashid bowed low, arms outstretched, as was the custom.

"Beg pardon, noble one, but my need is urgent. To the lands known as Mourning, I must travel, to the tower of one named Canticle."

Murk Dwellers
(The Dark, 4th Edition)

Beyond the tower, in the recesses of the marsh, ancient ruins came to life with the sounds of the awoken. Long sealed catacombs spat forth their contents, encrusted with the muck and filth of ages of neglect. Beneath the ashen sky, they crawled forth to the call of their master, a force as ancient and as powerful as the land itself.

Through sightless eyes, they sensed the world, their pallid, pale flesh rippling over long unused muscles. They entered the Mourning Lands, where they were so often known as ***Murk Dwellers****.*

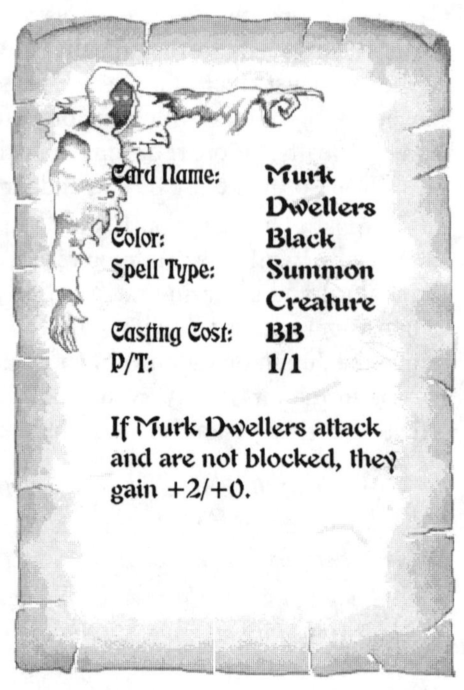

At a cost of 1 Black mana and 3 Colorless, these 2/2 creatures are deceptively powerful. When attacking, if they are unblocked, they gain +2/0.

Immediately obvious with these creatures are those tactics which render them unblockable: Dwarven Warriors and Tawnos's Wand, or lesser magicks such as Fear and Invisibility. All will function, allowing you to inflict an almost guaranteed 4 damage with every attack. And with the existence of Dark Ritual, they can be in play as early as the second turn. However, there are more subtle uses to which the Dwellers may be put, uses which may not be immediately obvious to the uninitiated.

Since there are few Magi who are keen on seeing the Murk Dwellers break through their defenses, a favored tactic is to place Venom on the Dwellers. The incentive to block is lowered, and the consequences of allowing them through remain the same. Augmenting the Dwellers with Firebreathing can be even more entertaining, since your opponent is now faced with a series of unpleasant choices. Block them, facing the inevitable destruction of the creature chosen for this task, or allow them through to inflict a wretched amount of damage.

Along the same lines, one can also use the Dwellers to force defending creatures into blocking in a less than ideal situation. When the choice is between blocking a Pit Scorpion or a Murk Dweller, a defender will not be thrilled at the prospects before him. Holding back Venomous Breath for a situation like this can be an excellent tactic. Once the defender is committed to blocking one, use Venomous Breath on that creature, removing the defending creature as a consideration in future attacks.

Placing Farrel's Mantle on Murk Dwellers can also be a wonderful way of getting rid of troublesome creatures. In one situation, I once had Murk Dwellers under the influence of Tawnos's Wand, bearing Farrel's Mantle. The result was an unblockable creature which would deal 4 damage to the opposing Mage, or 6 damage to any of his creatures. It was a wonderful setup requiring only three separate spells. Not an inconceivable situation at all.

Obviously, the utilitarian nature of Murk Dwellers makes them very popular targets for destructive magicks. Enchanting them with Holy Strength only prevents you from making them unblockable, so Holy Armor is a preferred choice. Ideally, the Murk Dwellers enter play early, in conjunction with the Dwarven Warriors, and cause large amounts of damage before they are annihilated. In a best case scenario, they can single-handedly secure a victory on the seventh turn. In a worst case scenario, they occupy an opponent's time and resources while you bring more problems into play.

Stumbling into the marsh, ruined cobbles crumbling beneath their step, they had no conception of what they had been summoned forth to accomplish. They knew only that they had to obey the call, an urge more telling than any they had felt in life, so long ago.

It had been so long since they had tasted the air, and they knew also that they did not wish to return to their dank and murky tombs.

Nether Shadow

(Alpha, Beta, Unlimited, Revised, 4th Edition)

Card Name: Nether Shadow
Color: Black
Spell Type: Summon Creature
Casting Cost: BB
P/T: 1/1

If three creatures are above Nether Shadow in graveyard, it can return to play during controller's upkeep. Shadow can attack the same turn as it enters and re-enters play.

The Specter drifted towards the tower, primitive thoughts wafting through the clouded remnants of its mind. Its lord and master had given it clear instructions, yet the closer it came to the tower which was its goal, the more distant and scrambled those instructions became. By the time the dwelling of the Necromancer was in sight, it knew only that it had to gain entry.

The granite facing of the tower was sparse, unadorned, the door magically warded against all forms of intrusion. Glyphs and sigils surrounded a small hole near the base of the tower, and words of power were etched on the edges of the chimney. Strangely, there seemed to be nothing preventing it from entering through the window. . . .

A hideous wail tore through the air as the Specter attempted entry, and it was confronted by the slate grey, spectral form of a ***Nether Shadow****.*

At a cost of 2 Black mana, this 1/1 creature is perhaps one of the most insidious in existence. When slain, most creatures are consigned to the graveyard until other magicks call them forth. The Nether Shadow returns to play at the end of your upkeep, however, so long as three other creatures are above it in the graveyard. As if this were not enough, the Shadow may attack on the turn it comes into play, as it does not suffer from summoning sickness.

The potential uses of the Nether Shadow are numerous and varied, and many are potent beyond imagining. Simply having 4 of them in your decks creates the potential for a limitless supply of blockers which will arrive under your control, every upkeep, so long as they continue to recycle themselves through your graveyard. This is, however, only the beginning.

Consider a first turn Dark Ritual. Using two to summon the Nether Shadow, the third mana can be used to place an Unholy Strength on the creature. Since it can attack on the turn summoned, you can immediately inflict 3 damage on your opponent. And on the next turn, when your foe is likely to have at best a */1 defender, it can attack yet again. In many instances, this combination can inflict a quick 6 points of damage before the duel has really even begun.

Even worse, consider the potential applications with those artifacts and creatures requiring sacrifices to function. Four Nether Shadows aren't even necessary if you're using Ashen Ghouls as well, since any combination between the four means a perpetual loop of creatures, continually coming into play during your upkeep. While the Ghouls require a payment of mana to return, it is minimal considering the benefits. Sacrifice them to the Fallen Angel, Ashnod's Altar, or the Life Chisel, and delight in the knowledge that they will return under your control the very next upkeep. If Enduring Renewal is in play, you don't even have to worry about bringing them into play in the first place—simply wait until enough creatures are discarded into your graveyard, and you can start bringing Nether Shadows back during your upkeep.

This brings into focus another aspect of the Nether Shadow: its application against Discard strategies. Most discard strategies rely on denial of cards and resources to defeat an opponent, possessing little in the way of extreme offensive capability as a result. Once Nether Shadows start entering your graveyard from either your hand or your library, you have access to resources which would have otherwise been denied. Again, when combined with Ashen Ghouls, this can be a potent weapon.

Getting rid of the Nether Shadow once and for all is somewhat more difficult. Simply burying or killing the Shadow is no guarantee that it will not return at some later date. Removing it from the game with Swords to Plowshares, or removing them from the graveyard with Night Soil or Tormod's Crypt are the only sure-fire methods of being rid of the beasts. All told, the Nether Shadow is an effective and troublesome beast.

The specter readied its ghostly lance and plunged it through the Nether Shadow, which appeared to melt around the shaft of the weapon. No sooner had it disappeared than another rose to take its place. The specter had no conception of what was happening, it knew only that it had to gain access to the tower. And so it continued its futile battle against the shadows.

It wasn't long before the specter itself disappeared, fading from existence as if it had never been, surrounded by the ashen forms of the shadows it had faced.

Paralyze

(Alpha, Beta, Unlimited, Revised, 4th Edition)

Card Name:	**Paralyze**
Color:	**Black**
Spell Type:	**Enchant Creature**
Casting Cost:	**B**
P/T:	**-**

Target creature doesn't untap as normal. Creature's controller may spend 4 to untap during upkeep. Tap target creature when Paralyze is cast.

Bandares clenched at the sill as he looked out over the ocean, eyes smouldering with fury. His voice was calm and measured, with an edge that would have put the fear of the elder spirits in anyone who heard it.

"Once more, for the record. Tell me why we're so far behind schedule? Unnatural weather you say?"

The bosun didn't flinch. He stood in front of the cabin door, arms folded behind his back, a slightly amused expression on his face. He didn't answer the lithe young mage, he simply stared in his general direction. Bandares turned on him, pointing an accusing finger.

"You know, I really thought this was going to be fun, but my patience is wearing a little bit thin. You've got, oh, three seconds to explain yourself before I start to toss off."

*The bosun, however, couldn't respond, for he had succumbed to the effects of **Paralyze**.*

A creature enchantment costing 1 Black mana, Paralyze taps the target creature when cast. From that point on, the creature fails to untap as it normally would. Instead, its controller must pay 4 mana during his or her upkeep to untap it.

On a variety of levels, Paralyze is an extremely effective enchantment, although many consider it inferior to spells which terminate or destroy creatures. However, there are numerous instances where a creature in play with a debilitating enchantment is far more effective than a creature in the graveyard.

For example, when faced with a variety of creatures which have nasty effects which are activated by tapping, Paralyze can serve to render them ineffective, without having to waste destructive energies on them. While a Prodigal Sorcerer may be annoying, and at times dangerous, there are creatures far more deadly which would be better targeted with a Terror. Paralyze effectively terminates the annoyance of the Sorcerer, since the untap cost will reduce resources your opponent may need to cast other spells. This works for a wide variety of creatures with tapping costs, including the Royal Assassin, the Samite Healer, the D'Avenant Archer, and a host of others.

This untap cost can also prove particularly potent when you are trying to keep an opponent from utilizing lands through methods such as land destruction, or better yet, the Winter Orb. Allow your foe to place a creature in play, and then cast Paralyze upon it. Once this has been done, put a Winter Orb into play, or destroy key lands. Now your enemy faces a crippling dilemma. Untap the only creature it has available for immediate use, which will prevent the casting of other spells, or cast other spells, facing the possibility of having them countered. In a Black/Blue Winter Orb deck, placing Paralyze on the first creature which comes into play can be the deciding maneuver.

Paralyze works in your favor should your creatures be affected by artifacts such as the Meekstone, or under the effect of spells which will not allow them to untap as normal. The effects of Ice Floe, Barl's Cage or Smoke can all be counteracted using Paralyze. Placing it on a creature afflicted by the Meekstone allows it to untap, period. Keeping things like this in consideration when selecting your spells is the difference between an apprentice and a master.

Bandares tapped his foot impatiently, glaring at the bosun all the while. Seconds passed like hours in the bosun's eyes, before the interminable wait was ended by a brief, mercifully painless flash of light.

The mage stood over a smouldering pile of ash, brushing his hands. Turning to his assistant, who was lying slumped in a hammock slung between two bulkheads, he nodded.

"Do clean this up before I get back. I'm going to have a word with the captain."

Pestilence

(Alpha, Beta, Unlimited, Revised, 4th Edition)

The narrow streets of Blacksand had always been less than sanitary. Buckets of filthy water and worse were continually dumped from the upper stories of overcrowded tenements, garbage collected in alleys, and the collected refuse of a thousand travellers wound up on the streets. This day, however, there was something new. Drunks normally slumped against the wall, sleeping off the effects of their binges. Now they were joined by the pox-ridden bodies of the dead and dying, for the streets of the great port city were rife with ***Pestilence****.*

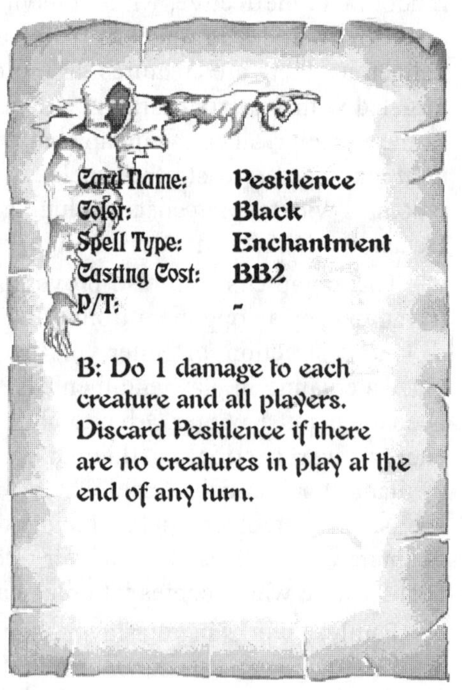

An enchantment which costs 2 Black and 2 Colorless mana to bring into play, Pestilence causes one damage to each player and creature for every 1 Black mana which is spent to activate it. If no creatures remain in play at the end of any turn, Pestilence is buried.

Pestilence is a spell which can be utilized on a variety of levels, all of which need to be analyzed to make full use of it. There are several different ways of activating it, which determine how it will be used. One can pump a large amount of mana into it doing one large chunk of damage all at once, or one can activate it several times over the course of a turn. Each tactic has its own benefits and uses.

When one is faced with a large number of creatures with considerable toughness, or a stalemate has been achieved, Pestilence can be used to wipe the slate clean in one blow, dealing four or five points of damage to everything and everyone in play. This tactic is best used when you have several regenerating creatures in your employ: while all of your opponents' creatures may end up in the graveyard, you will still have a Drudge Skeleton or two waiting on your side. This is also best used during your opponent's turn, giving you the chance to untap your regenerated creatures and the opportunity to bring more creatures into play. This use of Pestilence can also be extremely effective if a Khabal Ghoul or Scavenging Ghoul is brought into play immediately afterwards. Since these creatures gain counters based only on how many creatures died that turn and not when they died, they can quickly amass a great deal of power.

The second option involves using Pestilence in small 1-point bursts of damage. This is often used to overpower an individual using a Circle of Protection: Black, since he or she has to activate it each and every time you activate Pestilence. This is often a recommended tactic before launching an attack with superior numbers. In addition, casting Living Lands or using the Kormus Bell and then activating Pestilence can wipe out an opponent's lands. Protecting your own lands is a simple matter of using a spell like Castle. This same tactic works well against artifacts when a Xenic Poltergeist is active.

Obviously, options to protect your creatures and yourself from the effects of your own Pestilence should be taken. Circle of Protection: Black is obvious, while creatures may be protected by means of Black Ward. Unsummon is another option you may consider before using Pestilence. Regenerating creatures are always a good idea, while spells such as Blood of the Martyr and Reverse Damage may be used in combination to provide a nasty surprise for your opponent. While Pestilence is open to destruction by a wide variety of methods, it is usually capable of serving its purpose long before it has to fear for its existence.

Down the street, a single lantern bobbed in the darkness, wielded by a shaky and mottled hand. The young baker chanted slowly and softly to himself, a lament to the dead he had heard in his cradle. He staggered down the streets of the stricken city, singing it to himself over and over, certain that at some point he would fall victim to the plague. In the distance, the Beast stirred.

Scavenging Ghoul

(Alpha, Beta, Unlimited, Revised, 4th Edition)

The fields beyond the walls of Blacksand were being turned into makeshift cemeteries, entire families having been taken by the ravages of the plague. Carts bearing the dead were making continuous journeys towards abandoned farms, driven by individuals whose desire to loot the dead proved stronger than their instinct for survival. They were not the only ones interested in their grisly cargo, however. Stalking amidst the abandoned buildings of the farm, hiding behind mounds of freshly turned earth, there walked a ***Scavenging Ghoul****.*

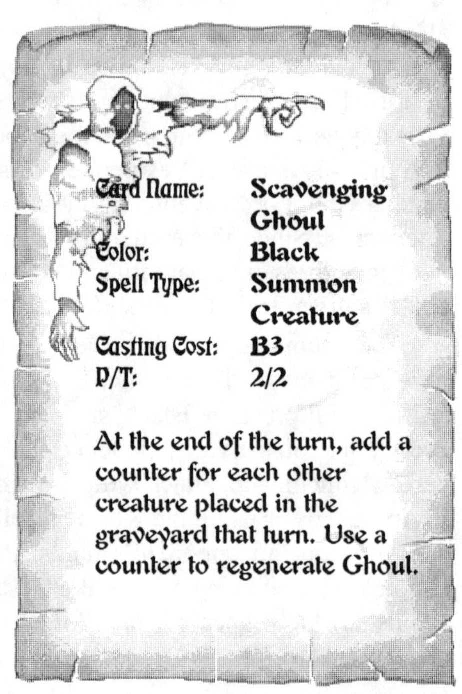

Card Name: Scavenging Ghoul
Color: Black
Spell Type: Summon Creature
Casting Cost: B3
P/T: 2/2

At the end of the turn, add a counter for each other creature placed in the graveyard that turn. Use a counter to regenerate Ghoul.

While this black 2/2 creature costs 1 Black mana and 3 Colorless to call forth, the ability it possesses is interesting enough to make it worth consideration. And the end of each turn, the Ghoul acquires a counter for every creature which was placed in the graveyard, even if the Ghoul was not in play at the time. If the Ghoul takes lethal damage, a counter may be removed in order to regenerate it.

Many people feel that the Ghoul is underpowered, since the regeneration ability it possesses is dependent on creatures being killed, as opposed to a simple activation cost. However, there are advantages to it as well. Rather than depending on the expenditure of mana, which may or may not be in plentiful supply, the Ghoul can always regenerate, so long as counters are present. This makes it a far more versatile defender, since you are not limited by your mana resources. A popular use of the Ghoul is in a deck which relies on numerous sacrifices and graveyard recycling, which includes the use of Ashen Ghouls and Nether Shadows. As creatures repeatedly enter the Graveyard, the Ghoul continues to acquire counters.

Obviously, a 2/2 regenerating creature can prove to be extremely valuable. Far more likely to kill off opposing creatures than a simple 1/1 skeleton, it also benefits from its immunity to Terror, a popular method of destroying Regenerators. If a large number of 1/1 creatures are in play, as the result of a Goblin deck or what have you, a single Pestilence will not only wipe them out, but also provide the Ghoul with even more regenerative opportunities. In addition, you are far more likely to attack with the Ghoul than with Drudge Skeletons or Walking Dead, as the 2/2 provides it with that much more offensive punch. So long as the Ghoul has counters, you have no need to husband mana reserves, or count your untapped lands, hoping to pull off a successful defense.

If one has access to Nevinyrral's Disk, even more destructive works can be performed. Once the Ghoul has acquired a counter, sweep the table using the Disk. The Ghoul may then be regenerated, acquiring a counter for every creature which was destroyed. This tactic will also work with spells such as Jokulhaups, or anything else which sends large numbers of creatures to the graveyard in one fell swoop.

Once the carts and their handlers had finished with their tasks, it was time for the Ghoul to engage in his. It was hardly an existence one would find appealing. . .robbing the graves of the dead, nourishing oneself on the remnants of life, skulking around in a state of perpetual unlife and ravenous hunger.

And yet it was an existence nonetheless, and for that the ghoul was thankful. And when the Beast walked Torwynn once again, the ghoul would serve it well.

Sorceress Queen

(Arabian Nights, Revised, 4th Edition)

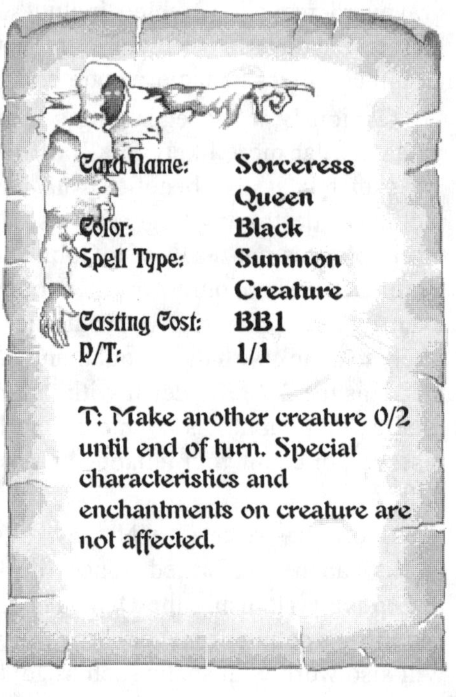

The sun rose over the domes and spires of Cameshbaan, greatest of the cities to be found in the South. The smells of wood smoke and spice hung over the market, as the merchants and travellers began the day with the haggling and trade which marked the routine of their lives.

Light filtered into the chamber through gauzy curtains, spilling out over the silk cushions and pillows which were scattered about the floor. The voices from the market echoed off the tiled, frescoed walls, clear and at the same time distant. She sat on a throne of ivory, painted nails tapping impatiently on the elaborately carved arm, her dark skin contrasting sharply with the surface on which she sat. Hassan had warned her, so long ago, of the dangers posed, and in her arrogance she had ignored him. Now, she had no choice but to listen, for she was first among the powers in the city, a ***Sorceress Queen****.*

2 Black mana and 1 Colorless will call forth this 1/1 creature, who with a tap can turn any creature other than herself into an 0/2 for the remainder of the turn.

The more immediate uses for this kind of ability are obvious. When you are on the attack, the Sorceress Queen can be used to reduce the effectiveness of blockers. The Wall of Swords which would have killed your Hill Giant will be killed instead, and without inflicting any damage. On the defensive, this tactic is equally effective. After an opponent has declared his attack, turn his or her largest attacking creature into a 0/2, blocking it with something just large enough to kill it. Alternately, the Sorceress Queen can be used to boost the defensive abilities of minor creatures, allowing them to survive in situations where they might otherwise fall. Changing a 1/1 into a 0/2 may be a decisive move, especially if you're using it to increase the overall toughness of creatures which have banded together.

Even outside of combat, the Sorceress Queen is eminently useful. Creatures which normally would survive the effects of a Lightning Bolt can be weakened; those which have had Weakness placed upon them can be killed. Note that the power of the Sorceress Queen is such that the numbers on the card are treated as being 0/2, so any placed enchantments make adjustments based on a rating of 0/2.

One of the most insidious uses of the Sorceress Queen is in conjunction with the Tracker. As the Tracker deals its power in damage to an opposing creature, it will easily destroy any creature which has been targeted by the Sorceress Queen. In addition, that creature will be unable to retaliate against the Tracker, as it has no power with which to do so. The combination is cheap (a Dark Ritual alone will bring out the Queen, and the Tracker costs only 3 mana total), effective, and will attract a great deal of attention. While requiring more component parts, simply having a few Prodigal Sorcerers available will produce much the same effect.

The Sorceress Queen, however, is extremely vulnerable to a wide variety of destructive magic, as it only has a toughness of one. It isn't even capable of altering its own statistics to protect itself, so alternate methods of keeping it alive will have to be found. Prismatic Ward is usually a good idea, or some form of enchantment to increase toughness. The Sorceress Queen is of significant enough power that one should try to keep it around as long as possible.

"Hessenti, do be a dear and gather my things. . . ."

A trembling servant, head shaved except for a single scalp lock, bowed before his mistress and rushed through the beaded curtain which lead into the hall.

"I dare say he's made things interesting. . .he always has, after all. Canticle, the Beast, and dear Hassan. . .who should I take care of first?"

Uncle Istvan
(The Dark, 4th Edition)

"Your taste in friends astounds me, Canty. . . ."

Ariana's comment was broken off as she began to cough, and she stopped to lean against the trunk of a long dead tree for support. They had been travelling through the fens and bogs of the Mourning Lands for the better part of a day, towards the northern borders with the Great Forest. Canticle shrugged at the comment, and simply pointed at the wigwam which was situated atop a muddy hillock.

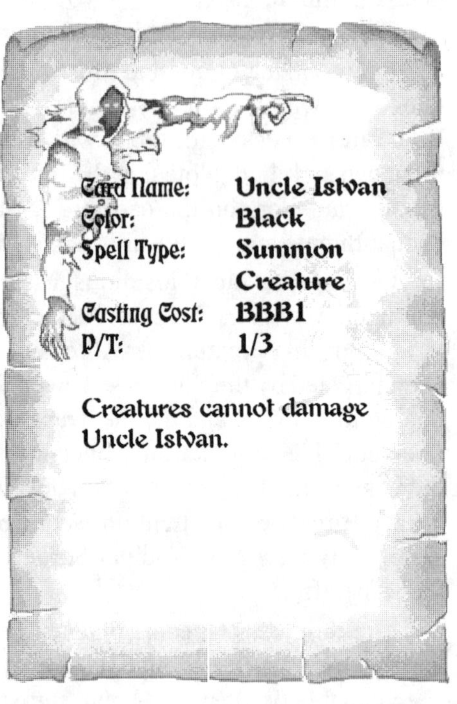

"We're almost there. . . ."

El-Hajjaj snorted, shoving aside a large pole which had been planted in the spongy earth. A skull mounted atop it wobbled with the movement.

"Barbaric as well. . .an ally like this we could do without."

Canticle almost smiled as he spoke.

"He's generally harmless, although his stability can be questioned. After all, he does call himself ***Uncle Istvan****."*

At a cost of 3 Black mana and 1 Colorless, this 1/3 creature seems rather an expensive investment. However, all damage which is done to Uncle Istvan by creatures is reduced to 0, which more than makes up for the high casting cost.

Obviously, this kind of ability makes Uncle Istvan the ideal blocker, especially if he has had Flight placed upon him, or has access to Arnjolt's Ascent. Creatures which have had Firebreathing placed upon them, the Shivan Dragon, or even the Hoar Shade are all rendered harmless when blocked by Uncle Istvan. Against creatures with

Trampling, or those who possess Rampage, Uncle Istvan's usefulness should be readily apparent.

One of the best ways to utilize Uncle Istvan, however, is in conjunction with a banding creature. When blocking, all damage can be assigned to Uncle Istvan, who will safely reduce that damage to 0. So long as a method exists of transferring damage from creatures to Uncle Istvan, you can safely carry out maneuvers which may have previously involved a great deal of risk.

Another favored tactic is the use of Venom on Uncle Istvan. No matter the size of the creature which Uncle Istvan blocks, it will fall before him. This combination, when combined with Lure, is absolutely devastating. Note the wording on Uncle Istvan as well. . .all damage dealt by creatures, with no reference to when they are dealing this damage. Thus, even creatures like the D'Avenant Archer and Prodigal Sorcerer will find their abilities less than useful, as the damage it inflicts will be reduced to 0.

As if all of this wasn't reason enough to utilize Uncle Istvan, consider the speed with which he can be brought into play. Despite the need for a large amount of specifically colored mana to summon him, Istvan can usually be brought into play by the second turn through the use of Dark Ritual. And a second turn 1/3 creature which takes no creature based damage can be decisive. Place Firebreathing on him, attack, and you can tie up valuable defenders for the duration of the duel.

When it comes to destroying Uncle Istvan, his wide and varied uses still come into play. Immune to Terror, his toughness generally doesn't allow the use of less destructive magicks. Lightning Bolt is an obvious avenue of approach, as is anything which clears out creatures indiscriminately (Wrath of God or Nevinyrral's Disk). There are few spellbooks that do not benefit from the presence of Uncle Istvan.

They were still some distance from the wigwam when a wild-haired old man burst forth from behind the ratty curtain which served as a door. Waving a blood-stained axe in one hand, bones and skulls dangling from the belt of his homespun tunic, he shouted obscenities and vile recriminations in a resonant voice. Canticle stood his ground and crossed his hands over his chest.

"Enough theatrics, we simply do not have the time."

Uncle Istvan looked as if he'd been struck by lightning, but slowly lowered his axe. The madness which had blazed within his eyes melted away in an instant, and he glared at the Necromancer.

"What is it you need. . . ."

Vampire Bats

(Legends, 4th Edition)

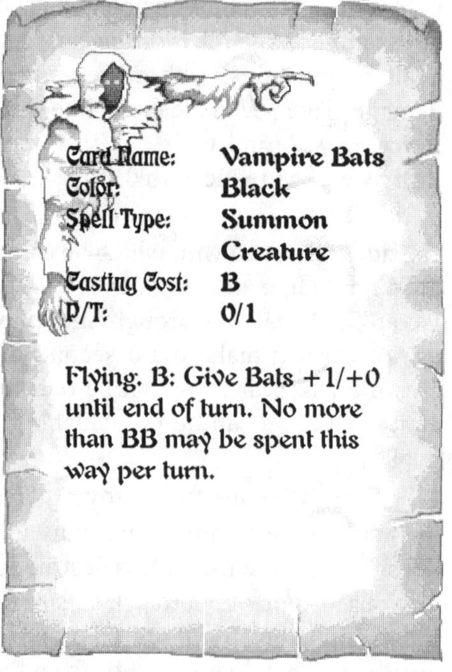

The wigwam was hardly what one would call comfortable. A matted collection of dirty straw and marsh reeds served as a bed, while a central firepit provided warmth and an eternally hazy, choking, atmosphere. A rickety wooden table was set up along one side, a collection of bloodied bones and pieces of unidentifiable flesh scattered across its surface. Uncle Istvan sat cross-legged on his bed, caressing the haft of his axe, speaking in low tones. Canticle, Ariana, and El-Hajjaj clustered around the fire, listening intently to his words.

"Oh, the Beast walks the lands he does, and in a fine mood indeed. Not exactly pleased with the way things turned out last time, to be sure. Finding the old codger, now that's the thing isn't it?"

Uncle Istvan snapped his fingers, and a high pitched chittering noise filled the interior of the wigwam. Dark shapes mounted on leathery wings took to the air, flying out of the smokehole into the night sky. Uncle Istvan kept many strange things in his hovel, not the least of them a flight of ***Vampire Bats****.*

A flying 0/1 creature costing 1 Black mana, the Vampire Bats may be pumped up +1/0 for every Black mana which is spent, until the end of the turn. The only drawback is that no more than 2 Black mana may be spent in this way during the course of a turn.

At such a low cost, the Vampire Bats are the ideal addition to any spellbook which emphasizes speed. A first turn Dark Ritual could bring out a Nether Shadow and the Vampire Bats, a pair of attackers which can deal a combined total of 3 damage by the second turn. As flying creatures go, they can serve adequately as attackers until the larger creatures come into play. Their primary advantage, however, is speed.

In a Black spellbook, the primary function of the Vampire Bats will be to provide air defense until the larger, more dangerous flying beasts can enter the fray. A first turn Vampire Bat will generally be able to hold off an aerial assault until the fourth or fifth turn, at which point a Fallen Angel or Sengir Vampire will generally be around to even up the odds. Since the Bats can be pumped to a level of 2/1, they're generally effective as defenders for a period of three or four turns. In addition, should your opponent lack flying defenses, he can repeatedly launch attacks with a power of 2 that will slowly whittle away at his life points. Nor is one required to pump up the Bats at all. If you are safe from aerial assault, and you would be better served by an additional attacker, it may be best to use the 2 Black mana to summon another Nether Shadow or work towards the casting of destructive magicks.

Even in the later stages of a duel, when most lesser creatures have generally outlived their usefulness, the Vampire Bats can be put to good use. A favored use is with the Sorceress Queen. When an attack is declared, use the Queen to turn an opposing Flyer into a 0/2. The Bats can then make short work of it and still survive. Even if they are used as sacrificial blockers, they can still bring a Serra Angel down to the point where a Lightning Bolt or even Pyroclasm will take it out.

While the Vampire Bats are generally overlooked due to their fragile nature, they cannot be underestimated. In a spellbook which emphasizes speed, they can be invaluable, as they can be brought out early and enchanted by means of Unholy Strength, in effect providing a 4/2 flyer by the third turn. Properly used, the Vampire Bats can be a deciding factor in a duel.

Uncle Istvan chuckled as the last of the bats winged its way forth into the night, and he kissed the blade of his axe.

"Oh, find him they shall, and then what will you do? Dance beneath the stars in his embrace? Heh, no, no. . . ."

Ariana began to cough, which sent wracking shudders down her fragile frame. Canticle looked over in concern, though his words were clearly directed at Uncle Istvan.

"When this is over, the debt is paid in full."

Putting his arm around Ariana, the Necromancer led her from the wigwam. El-Hajjaj followed close behind, a look of barely concealed disgust on his face. As they entered the Marsh, he spat on the ground.

"Does that man never bathe?"

Weakness

(Alpha, Beta, Unlimited, Revised, 4th Edition)

"Now Captain, I'm sure you're beginning to see things my way, aren't you?"

Bandares sat in the high backed Captain's chair, drumming his fingers on the mahogany surface of the desk. His assistant sat atop a large sheaf of papers, adjusting his cap while scratching at the tip of his blunt nose. The Captain was writhing on the floor, clutching at his chest while trying to respond.

"What was that? I can't quite hear you. . . .dreadfully sorry, it's one of the side effects of ***Weakness****."*

Card Name:	Weakness
Color:	Black
Spell Type:	Enchant Creature
Casting Cost:	B
P/T:	-

Target creature loses -2/-1.

This creature enchantment costs a mere 1 Black mana, and saps a target creature's strength, putting it at -2/-1, and is an effective method of reducing an opponent's offensive and defensive capabilities.

While many individuals choose Terror over Weakness due to the more permanent nature of destruction, Weakness can serve a variety of useful purposes when properly applied. In a wide variety of situations, Weakness can be applied to a creature you wish to keep in play, but rendered ineffective in combat. These include creatures which have had Wanderlust played on them, creatures with expensive upkeep costs, such as the Minion of Tevesh Szat, or creatures which harm their controller such as the Serendib Efreet. In desperate situations, Weakness can even be used to kill creatures which have a toughness of one. In addition, when placed on the Hypnotic Specter and The Fallen, Weakness prevents those creatures from utilizing their special abilities. Against a Black Mage, Weakness is often an excellent substitution for Terror.

Weakness can also serve as a fallback when other methods of dealing with creatures simply aren't proving effective. Tossing a Weakness on a Serra Angel can allow you to Lightning Bolt it. Using a Weakness on one of your creatures which has had Creature Bond placed upon it can lessen the impact of its destruction. Slightly more complex is using Weakness and then Transmutation to take out a creature or reduce its overall power.

There are even more esoteric situations in which Weakness can prove worthwhile, however. For example, consider the situation when a Meekstone is in play, and no creature with a toughness greater than 2 can untap. Toss a Weakness on one of your 4/* or 3/* creatures to allow it the opportunity to launch an attack. This tactic works particularly well with the Fallen Angel. When Weakness is placed on it, you can use the other creatures which are unable to untap as sacrifices to boost its power and toughness.

The captain simply expired on the floor of his cabin, a tiny trickle of blood emerging from his mouth. His hat, a symbol of authority, was firmly grasped in one hand, his other still clutching at his chest. Bandares stood up, and walked over to the corpse.

"Tsk, you'd think they'd be made of sterner stuff. . . ."

He reached over and pried the captain's hat from his hands, placing it atop his head.

"We've got ourselves a ship, my friend. I think it's time we used it."

Xenic Poltergeist
(Antiquities, 4th Edition)

The Lord of the Mountain entered the farmhouse, discovering to his dismay that there was no one about. He set his goblin assistant to the task of recording the contents of the hovel and began to make the rounds.

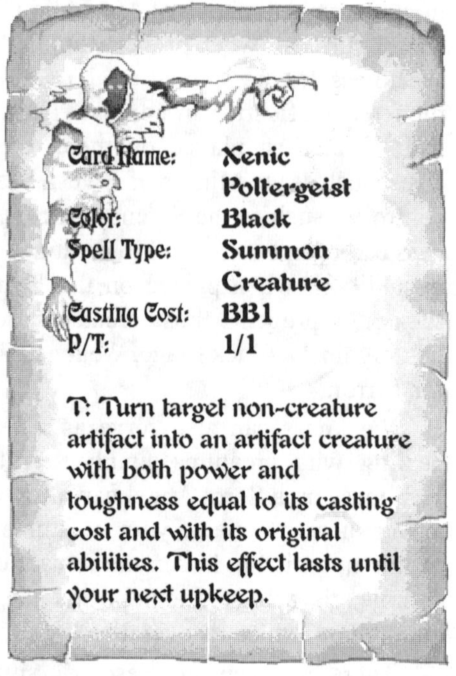

Sighing, he sat down at the table, putting his head in his hands.

"What a day."

A high-pitched keening noise caught his attention, and he turned around. The goblin scribe leapt under the table just in time to avoid a hurtling bronze projectile which flew from the mantle. The Beast was at play yet again, having unleashed a ***Xenic Poltergeist****.*

A 1/1 creature costing 2 Black mana and 1 Colorless, the Poltergeist possesses the ability to animate artifacts. When tapped, any non-creature artifact can be turned into a beast with a power and toughness equal to its casting cost until your next upkeep. The target artifact retains all of its regular abilities as well.

One of the more popular uses of the Xenic Poltergeist is against opposing artifacts which have no casting cost. Moxen, the Dark Sphere, the Fountain of Youth and the Zuran Orb can all be destroyed simply by tapping the Poltergeist and animating the artifact. With a toughness of 0, the newly created creature is slain.

The Poltergeist can also be used effectively against opposing artifacts which don't have a 0 casting cost. Use it against something with a considerable casting cost, such as Pyramids or Aladdin's Lamp. Place a Creature Bond on the newly created creature, then proceed to destroy it. While this effectively requires three cards, it is a devastating combination. If Detonate is used as the destructive force in the combination, it is even more devastating. Using the Xenic Poltergeist on lower cost artifacts such as the Throne of Bone allows you to get rid of them by means of the Prodigal Sorcerer or the Rod of Ruin.

Another common use for this creature is in the creation of an attacker or defender for a turn. The larger artifacts that have started to lose their utility in a duel can be used as fuel in an assault, or as a sacrificial defender to shore up a crumbling line. Better still, use it on Artifacts which can be sacrificed to provide a benefit. For example, animate the Aeolipile, declare it as a blocker, and before damage is dealt, sacrifice it to deal damage to a target of your choice. In other instances, the Xenic Poltergeist can animate those artifacts which are beginning to prove a hindrance, making it easier for you to get rid of them. If the Ankh of Mishra has ceased to serve a useful function, animate it and declare it as a defender. This tactic also serves well with artifacts that have been negatively enchanted in some way, whether it is by Warp Artifact or Artifact Possession.

Since the newly created creature retains all of its previous abilities, however, it can be of incredible utility when used on the defensive. Cursed Rack, Mightstone and similar artifacts continue to generate their effects, while at the same time serving as defenders. It's bad enough when you've animated your Weakstone to provide a 4/4 defender, but it's even worse when that defender is giving all attackers a -1/0 penalty.

While highly susceptible to destructive magicks, the Xenic Poltergeist can be useful in a wide range of spellbooks. Even if your opponent is not using artifacts, your own artifacts may be all you need. While hardly ideal in all situations, it is something which should be given due consideration.

The Lord of the Mountain ducked, reaching under the table as the bronze missile hurtled by yet again. Swinging around for another pass at the Mage, it began its approach.

CLANG

The missile dropped to the floor as it impacted with the cooking pan which the Lord of the Mountain had pulled from under the table. Brushing his hands, he got to his feet and pulled his cowering scribe from his hiding place.

"I do think it's time someone did something about all this foolishness.

Blue Spells

Apprentice Wizard

(The Dark, 4th Edition)

"We are not talking surgery here. I simply require an assistant slightly more skilled in the magical arts than my friend over there."

Bandares pointed to the leathery, impish creature which was straddling a sea chest, picking at its wispy beard. It waved at the trembling seaman, winking.

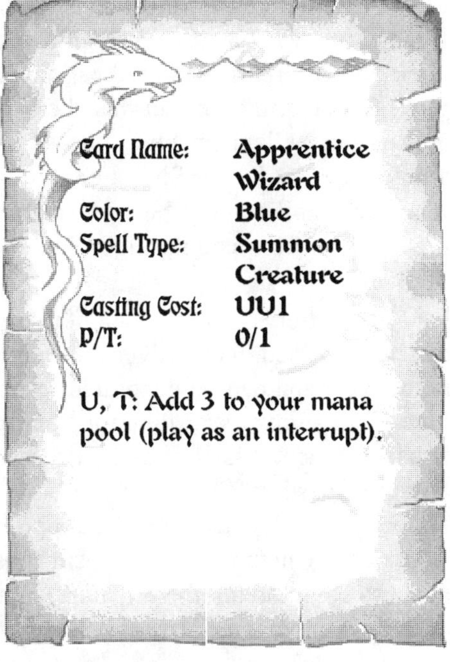

The seaman, a sallow-faced youth with sunken eyes and stringy brown hair, trembled. He had seen what Bandares was capable of and had no desire to cross him. How could he explain that he knew nothing of magic?

*"Now see here. I don't need any objections. What I do need is an **Apprentice Wizard**."*

At a cost of 2 Blue and 1 Colorless mana, the 0/1 Apprentice Wizard is an excellent investment. When it is tapped and 1 blue mana paid, 3 Colorless mana are added to your pool as an interrupt.

Although its initial cost may dissuade many from utilizing this creature as a source of fast mana, the benefits which it provides simply cannot be discounted. When the activation cost is paid, you are in essence receiving three mana for the price of one. If Instill Energy has been played on the Apprentice Wizard, you could even generate 6 mana with the expenditure of 2 blue. The applications are boundless.

Assuming a third turn Apprentice Wizard, by the fourth turn you will have access to a minimum of 5 mana. In the classic Blue spellbook, woefully devoid of fast mana, this can be a decisive amount. The Air Elementals which have had to wait until the fifth or sixth turn can be out that much earlier.

As if access to fast mana was not enough, consider the applications when used in conjunction with other colors. With Black, the Colorless mana from the Apprentice Wizard can be funneled through the Initiates of the Ebon Hand, allowing you to increase the power of a Drain Life. With Red, more Colorless mana means larger and more powerful Fireballs, Lava Bursts, and Disintegrates. Even in a mono Blue spellbook, the Apprentice Wizard can increase the effectiveness of Power Sink. Considering the fact that the best defense against counterspells are counterspells themselves, the Apprentice Wizard can also provide a buffer against Power Sink, Force Spike or the use of Vodalian Mage. Since this ability may be used as an Interrupt, there is nothing to prevent you from countering a Power Sink with the required amount of mana.

As mentioned earlier, each of these uses, apart from the Interrupts, can be increased in effectiveness with the simple use of Instill Energy. Now, six mana can be generated in one turn, simply by expending 2 blue. This allows you far more options in spellcasting. Consider a situation where 4 Islands and a Forest are in play. You know have the option of casting 2 spells which have a total cost of 4 or 5 mana, as opposed to only one. Tap the Apprentice Wizard, and cast Ray of Command. Untap the Wizard using Instill Energy, and you can tap it again to summon another creature. With this kind of mana advantage over your opponent, it won't be long before he or she surrenders.

The biggest disadvantage to the Apprentice Wizard is its vulnerability. Any spell or effect designed to inflict damage will take it out, and there really isn't much that can be done to prevent it, apart from protective enchantments. Using the mana advantage it provides as soon as possible is usually the wisest course of action, as there is little you can do to insure its long term survival.

Bandares stood up and put his arm around the youth, smiling in a disturbing fashion.

"Oh come now, don't look so distraught. We'll be in Easthold soon, and then we'll have some real fun. That's what being an apprentice is all about, after all. . . ."

Boomerang

(Legends, Chronicles)

"I knew this was a bad idea from the moment we set out."

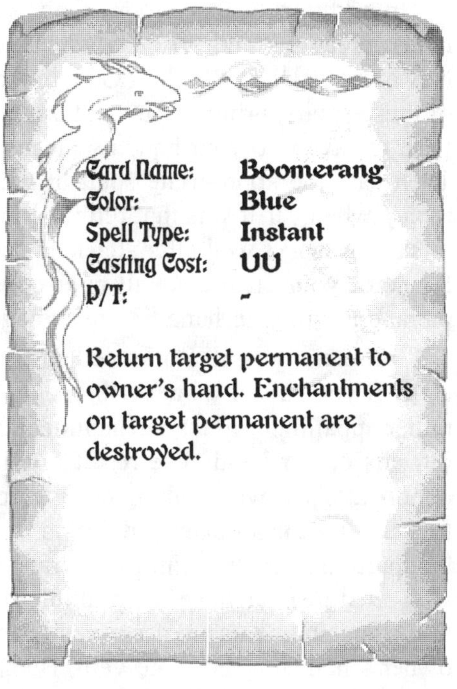

Ariana winked at Canticle as he turned to glare at her. This trek to the home of the Lord of the Mountain had indeed been his idea, but it was the only way he had to insure that the mercurial Mage would keep himself out of the way during this contest. The last time the Beast had walked Torwynn, the fool had refused even to acknowledge its existence, insisting that it had been a publicity stunt on the part of the Necromancer.

And now he stood on the trail leading to the Lord of the Mountain's abode, facing the wrought iron gate with the grinning gargoyle atop it. And true to form, the gargoyle spoke.

"Before the other side ye see. . . ."

Canticle gesticulated wildly, and a blue aura surrounded the Gargoyle. With a self-satisfied smirk, the Necromancer sent it back to its creator with a ***Boomerang****.*

Costing only 2 Blue mana, this Instant returns a target permanent to the owner's hand. As with any card that leaves play, any enchantments on that permanent are then buried.

One of the most effective uses of Boomerang is in getting rid of detrimental enchantments which are afflicting your land. Psychic Venom, Phantasmal Terrain, Cursed Land, Blight and numerous other enchantments can all be removed by means of Boomerang. Simply return the land to your hand, and the Enchantment is removed. The land can then be safely replayed. This tactic works equally well with creatures which have been afflicted with Wanderlust, Creature Bond or similar such nastiness. Simply Boomerang them back into your hand and recast them.

In addition to this, Boomerang is also an excellent way to save lands, creatures and artifacts which would otherwise fall victim to Nevinyrral's Disk, Wrath of God, or Armageddon. Before casting any of these spells, bring those creatures, enchantments and artifacts you wish to save into your hand by means of Unsummon or Boomerang. Then cast the appropriate spell of mass destruction. Then recast or replay whatever it was that returned to your hand. To a lesser extent, this tactic works well after attackers and blockers have been declared. If one of your creatures will be irretrievably destroyed, simply Boomerang it into your hand before damage is resolved.

Boomerang is also of excellent use against your opponent, especially if you have a Winter Orb in play. After your foe has cast a large, rather appalling artifact, enchantment, or creature, Boomerang it back into his or her hand. The result is a lot of expended mana on your opponent's part with nothing to show for it. With a Winter Orb in play, this also means an extended period of time before he or she can cast that particular spell again. Boomerang is also an effective way to deal with creatures that have had multiple enchantments placed upon them, as the enchantments are destroyed when the creature is returned to the owner's hand. In the same vein, Boomerang can be used to destroy token permanents. When an opponent Control Magics your Air Elemental, for example, Boomerang is one of the quickest ways to get it back.

On the offensive side of things, Boomerang is best utilized during the attack. When an opponent with a wide variety of Circles of Protection declares that he or she is not blocking, confident in the power of that Circle of Protection: Blue, simply Boomerang the Circle. Now, your Mahamoti Djinn has free reign to wreak havoc.

Canticle and his group continued up the mountain trail, the Necromancer delighted with the results of his spell. All trace of amusement disappeared from his face as they rounded the corner and faced the ubiquitous mailbox which was planted on the edge of the trail. A large, hand-painted sign hung from it. Though the writing was rushed and haphazard, the message was clear: "Gone Fishing".

The Necromancer ran his hands through his hair as Ariana chuckled softly to herself.

"I really do hate that man."

Creature Bond

(Alpha, Beta, Unlimited, Revised, 4th Edition)

"Don't take another step. . . ."

Seaman though he once may have been, the power shown to him by Bandares had changed him in ways he hadn't thought possible. Now he stood before Dardinel, the mate, and ordered him as if he was a cabin boy. And the mate obeyed.

"Now, listen very carefully. I want you to close your eyes, and jump."

"But Siward. . . ."

"DO IT!"

*Dardinel swallowed, and leapt off the plank into the churning waters of the Easthold straights. He wouldn't live long, but the death promised to be more swift than others Siward offered. Little did he know that Bandares' apprentice was using him to test a **Creature Bond**.*

Card Name:	**Creature Bond**
Color:	**Blue**
Spell Type:	**Enchant Creature**
Casting Cost:	**U1**
P/T:	**-**

If target creature goes to the graveyard, do damage equaling creature's toughness to creature's controller.

A potent creature Enchantment costing 1 Blue and 1 Colorless, Creature Bond is insidious indeed. When the creature that this spell enchants is destroyed, it deals an amount of damage to its controller equal to its toughness.

The more blatantly obvious uses for this spell are dangerous enough. Before casting Terror, Fissure, or any other creature destroying spell, simply place Creature Bond on the beast. Creature Bond can also be used as an effective deterrent on attacking creatures. Ironroot Treefolk won't be nearly as effective on the attack if an opponent believes them to be at risk of being destroyed. Rather than attack, he or she may simply hold them back.

There are numerous ways, however, of increasing the lethality of Creature Bond. One of the most elegant and cruel is using beneficial enchantments on your opponents' creatures. Putting a Creature Bond on a Serra Angel is bad enough. Then add Holy Armor, pump it up, and cast Terror. Holy Strength, Unholy Strength, and even Giant Growth can all be used to perform this sort of operation on an opposing creature.

If you want things to get even more vicious, cast Creature Bond on an artifact creature, and then utilize Detonate. If Detonate isn't available, Disenchant works almost as well, it simply allows for less damage. A more cunning way of inflicting damage is to use the Xenic Poltergeist on your foe's artifact creatures, Creature Bond them, and then destroy them. Animate Artifact can be used in much the same way, although has a higher cost in terms of resources. Another method of creating artifact creatures for use with Detonate is by means of Ashnod's Transmogrant. . .not only will you have an artifact creature, but you'll have a slight increase in damage as a result of the Creature Bond as well. Chandler could also be used to destroy a Bonded artifact creature quickly and easily, although there would be no additional benefits as with Detonate.

If you want to create further dilemmas for your opponent, slap a Wanderlust on a Wall, and then Creature Bond it. Your opponent will be in a situation where he will want to destroy the Bonded creature, but cannot do so without inflicting damage upon himself.

In order to avoid having the Creature Bond disenchanted or removed as a result of Tranquility, it is usually best to place it on a creature the turn you intend on destroying it. Unless you are planning to use the Creature Bond as a deterrent, there is little reason to delay the inevitable, after all.

Siward waited a few moments before turning his attention to one of the sailors hauling in sail. Bandares stepped out of the Captain's cabin just as the unfortunate sailor clutched at his head and began to scream. There was an audible explosion, and he fell to the deck. Siward winced, thankful that the ropes and mast blocked his view of the entire scene. Bandares simply chuckled.

"Not bad at all. You'll do quite well."

Feedback

(Alpha, Beta, Unlimited, Revised, 4th Edition)

A chill wind swept over the Mourning Lands, carrying with it the sting of the coming winter. Along with it, ash and soot settled on stagnant pools of water. In the mountains, the volcano continued to spew forth its contents.

*A man in red robes lay outside the door to Canticle's tower, clutching at his stomach. The scent of ozone hung in the air, and the edges of his garment were laced with powder burns. Sent by Bandares to delay the Necromancer, the stripling mage had fallen victim to **Feedback**.*

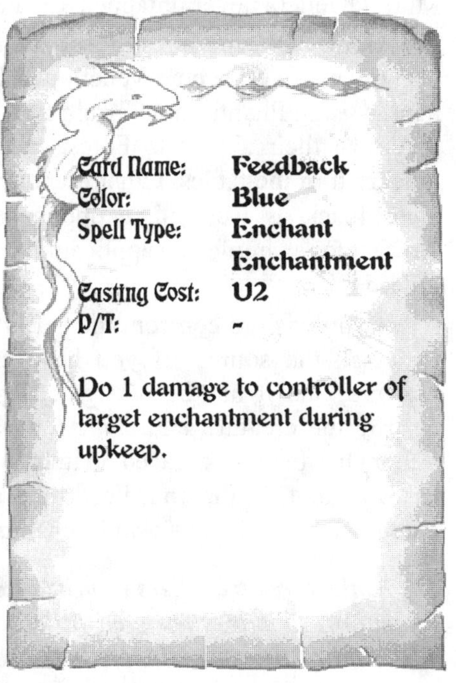

This 1 Blue mana, 2 Colorless mana Enchantment can be placed on any other Enchantment in play. Feedback then does 1 damage to the controller of the targeted Enchantment during his or her upkeep. A simple yet effective design.

The uses this spell has against beneficial enchantments are readily apparent on even cursory examination. Using Feedback on long-term Enchantments such as Powerleech, Lifetap, Energy Flux and Haunting Wind puts your foe in a position where he or she is forced to choose between taking damage or destroying the Enchantment altogether. Placing Feedback on Circles of Protection is a favorite method of tying down resources as well: if a Circle of Protection: Blue exists, it has to deal with Feedback before anything else.

Feedback can also be used to persuade an opponent to remove detrimental enchantments from your creatures, as enchantments remain controlled by their caster, no matter where they are placed. Demonic Torment, Spirit Shackle, Paralyze are all under the control of your opponent and so when Feedback is placed deal damage to your opponent. Once placed, a great deal of incentive exists for your opponent to remove them in some manner. In one instance, a Feedback was placed on a Paralyze which afflicted Murk Dwellers. Ultimately, as the Murk Dwellers never untapped, the Feedback killed the opponent.

Along the same lines, Feedback is incredibly useful against Enchantments like Psychic Venom and Phantasmal Terrain. If an opponent is using Phantasmal Terrain to allow his or her Shanodin Dryads to utilize their ability to Forestwalk, Feedback on the Terrain can quickly turn the tables. Other combinations scream for the placing of a Feedback as well. If an opponent uses Control Magic or Steal Artifact for example, the application of Feedback can be sweet revenge indeed.

If you wish to confront the perils of Feedback, the easiest way is to attack the source. If you have cast Weakness on an opposing creature, and it has been targeted by Feedback, find some way to destroy the creature entirely. Along a similar vein, if your Psychic Venom has feedback placed on it, try to destroy the land rather than the Enchantment. In the end, Feedback can be deadly if you aren't prepared to deal with your own Enchantments.

As the three travellers returned from their quest to the Lord of the Mountain's abode, they paid little attention to the body which was sprawled at the entrance to the Tower. In times such as these, such occurrences were far less a surprise than one might expect.

It wasn't long before the door to the tower opened yet again. Four gremlins scrambled outside, hopping and leaping over each other with wild abandon, giggling all the while. Spotting the body, they each took hold of a limb and carried it off, deep into the Marsh.

Flash Flood

(Legends, Chronicles)

Card Name: **Flash Flood**
Color: **Blue**
Spell Type: **Instant**
Casting Cost: **U**
P/T: **-**

Destroy red permanent or return mountain to owner's hand. Destroy enchantments on target land.

On the western shores of Easthold, villages dot the coastline. The inhabitants eke out a living on fish and whaling, hoping against hope that the seasons and the spirits of weather don't conspire to bring yet another storm down upon them.

Disaster arrives from a completely unexpected quarter on this day. The quiet, pebbled banks of the Loneshell River provide the first hint of trouble, frothing and bubbling in a disturbing manner as the waters rush out to the ocean. It's simply a curiosity for the townsfolk, however, who gather by the bridge to watch the display. A dull roar, approaching from the mountains, is their only warning, and by then it is too late. The waters crash down upon the bridge, and the village is caught by the rage of a ***Flash Flood****.*

A 1 Blue mana Instant, the power of Flash Flood allows you to destroy a target red permanent, or return a target mountain to its owner's hand. Any Enchantments on this target Mountain are destroyed.

In its simplest form, Flash Flood provides a Blue Mage with yet another method to wipe out the armies of Red. Using Blue Elemental Blasts to counter spells, Flash Flood can be used to take out those Red permanents which actually make it into play. Cheaper than Terror, Flash Flood is an ideal anti-creature spell when you're facing someone who makes heavy use of Red spells. There are far more ways to take advantage of Flash Flood, however.

Not only can you use Flash Flood to return an opponent's mountain to his or her hand, effectively setting them back in resources, but you can do this with your own Mountains as well. If your Mountain has been enchanted by Psychic Venom or Cursed Land, Flash Flood can be the ideal way of getting rid of the enchantment without losing the land. Given the relative lack of anti-enchantment magicks available to Blue, this is definitely something which should be given due consideration. This anti-enchantment aspect of Flash Flood is also useful when your opponent is using things like Earthlore or Wild Growth on his or her lands.

Another aspect of Flash Flood that should be kept in mind is its application against Gold Enchantments and Legends that have Red mana as part of their casting cost. These spells and creatures are just as susceptible to the effects of Flash Flood as something which requires only Red mana. A variation on this theme is to use Flash Flood to deny Mountains which may be necessary for the payment of upkeep costs. Take Rohgahh of Kher Keep, for example. If your opponent has three mountains, use Flash Flood to take out one of them. Rohgahh then switches allegiance, becoming an asset to you rather than a liability. In battle, Flash Flood can be used after an attack has been declared to remove Mountains which may otherwise be used to Regenerate that Uthden Troll.

Timbers, trees, boulders. . .everything in the path of the churning waters was uprooted, thrown into the air, and brought down into the frothing maelstrom of the river. The villagers had seconds to make peace with the spirits before they were carried off into the next life, while animals and livestock stood rooted in terror before the waves fell down upon their fields. In a matter of seconds, the village was but a memory.

High in the mountains above the village, laughter echoed across an ancient valley. The Beast walked Torwynn once again.

Giant Tortoise
(Arabian Nights, 4th Edition)

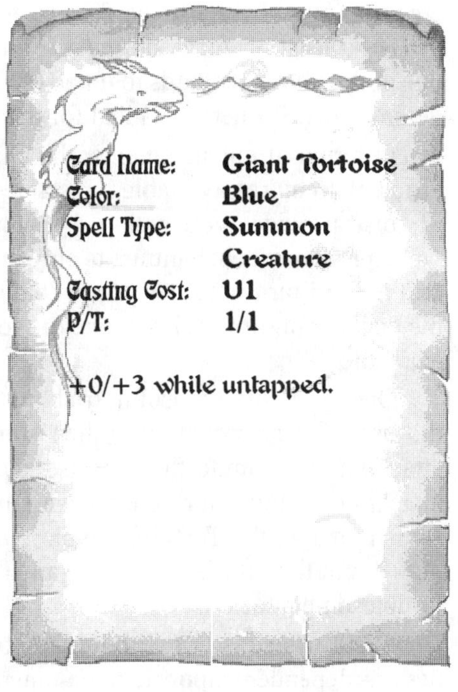

Deep within the heart of the marsh, amidst brackish pools of algae-encrusted waters and tall stands of cattails, the Lord of the Mountain sat down atop a muddy hill. His eyes seemed focused on the efforts of a gang of gremlins, trying awkwardly to deal with the body they had carried into the Marsh.

"Just a little bit closer. . . ."

Even as the words left his lips, the mound atop which he sat began to shift and move. From beneath a fallen log, a tremendous eye opened, glaring at the gremlins and their gruesome burden. The Gremlins dropped the body and scattered into the Marsh, while the Lord of the Mountain urged his mount forward. The gremlins wailed and screeched, pursued through the Marsh by a ***Giant Tortoise****.*

A simple 1/1 beast that can be summoned with 1 Blue mana and 1 Colorless, there is far more to this creature than one might expect. So long as the Tortoise is untapped, confined within its armored shell, it gains 0/+3, effectively rendering it a 1/4 creature.

It is this ability which makes the Tortoise one of the most cost-effective defenders available. With a power of only 1, the urge to use this creature in an offensive capability is far from great, and to tap it would render its special ability worthless. The wise simply leave the Tortoise in place and allow it to function as a permanent 1/4 defender. In this way, for only 2 mana you gain a creature which is effectively immune to Lightning Bolt and which can safely confront any land-based creature you're likely to encounter in the early stages of a duel.

If one has access to Twiddle, the Elder Druid or Jandor's Saddlebags, the Giant Tortoise can become even more useful. If the opponent hasn't the means to block or destroy the Tortoise, or has committed his creatures elsewhere, use the Tortoise to attack, tossing a Giant Strength or Blood Lust on for good measure. Once the attack is resolved, use one of the above methods to untap the Tortoise, making it available for defense. Instill Energy is ideal for this sort of tactic.

In terms of enhancements, the Giant Tortoise is one of the more efficient creatures available. Unstable Mutation on a defending Giant Tortoise provides you with a 4/7 blocker as early as the third turn, while permanent enchantments only make it deadlier. Unholy Strength on the third turn provides you with a 3/5 defender for the duration of the duel (or until it is slain), one of the cheapest power-to-mana ratios available.

One particularly useful trick with the Giant Tortoise involves the use of Transmutation. When something particularly noxious is attacking, Transmute the Tortoise and assign it to block. Where the attacking creature may once have simply lost the opportunity to do some damage, the Tortoise which is now 4/1 could kill it. Though it may die in the process, it can be an effective method of eliminating a troublesome attacker.

The Tortoise is not without drawbacks. Since the boost to toughness is dependent upon it remaining untapped, any artifact or spell which taps can quickly render the Tortoise useless, as well as vulnerable to the effects of the Prodigal Sorcerer or Rod of Ruin. The Icy Manipulator, Twiddle, or even Riptide can quickly bring an end to the Giant Tortoise.

Standing atop the Tortoise, barely able to keep his balance, the Lord of the Mountain motioned to his goblin assistant, who was perched atop the beast's head. The goblin nodded and steered the Tortoise in the direction of a distant tower.

"I do wonder if Canticle likes pets . . . . "

Jump

(Alpha, Beta, Unlimited, Revised, 4th Edition)

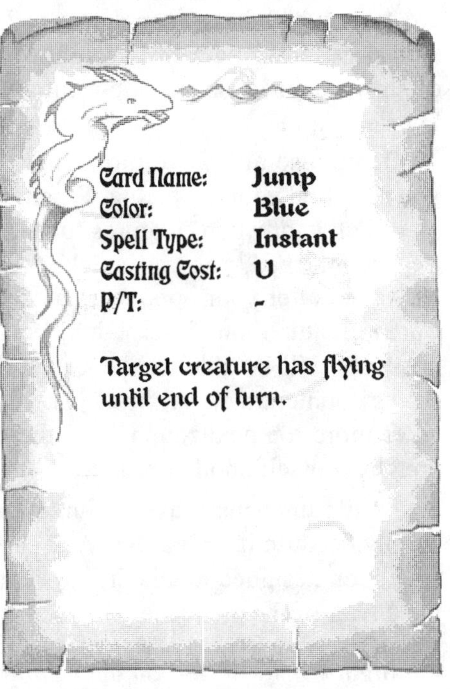

Aboard the Devil Dancer, things hadn't improved. Bandares was occupied in his quarters with some new form of magick, once again leaving Siward in charge of running the ship. And for the fledgling apprentice, it was an opportunity to hone his new-found abilities.

Looking upwards, he noticed that Sigurd had taken watch in the crow's nest. Siward had never liked Sigurd, a crass and crude caricature of a sailor if ever there was one. And now he had his opportunity to do something about it.

"Sigurd!"

The man in the crow's nest looked down, spitting over the side as he did so. A damp wad of tobacco landed right next to Siward. Closing his eyes and focusing his concentration, Siward shouted.

*"**JUMP!**"*

At a cost of 1 Blue mana, this Instant is an often overlooked piece of work. When cast, a target creature gains Flying until the end of the turn. Many have argued that with the existence of Flight, this spell has little application. Not so.

One of the most common uses for Jump is for the surprise factor during an attack or on defense. When an opponent declares an attack, thinking his or her Serra Angel safe from your ground-based forces, simply toss Jump on your Glacial Wall. Better still, cast it on a creature like the Abomination. Not only will it survive the impact with the Serra Angel, it will destroy it as well. Some of the most effective uses for Jump, however, involve using it on your opponents' creatures.

A personal favorite use for Jump involves what is called "skeet-shooting." After tossing Jump on an opposing creature, use the Grape-shot Catapult to bring it down. Alternately, you could use Earthbind on creatures which have a toughness of 2 or less, although this tends to be a desperation maneuver. If you have multiple Jumps in hand, cast all of them at once on an opponent's creatures and follow it up with Hurricane.

Jump also allows you to avoid one of the deadlier combinations you may find yourself facing. When the Thicket Basilisk has had Lure placed on it, or when creatures such as Uncle Istvan have had Lure and Venom attached, you can quickly find yourself bereft of defenders. However, after your opponent has declared his or her attack with the Lured creature, simply cast Jump on it. None of your ground-based creatures will be able to block it, freeing them up for a rather monstrous counterattack. At best, you take 2 damage and your opponent takes more the next round from the counterattack. At worst, you've bought yourself another round.

While Jump may have its limitations, it should never be discounted simply because it isn't a "power" card. It has its uses, especially in a spellbook designed to take it into consideration. Never underestimate the power of the mundane.

Sigurd hung in the air momentarily, like an immense, awkward bird. Flapping his arms madly, flailing his legs, his valiant attempts to return to his perch failed. Landing with a sickening crunch next to Siward, he managed a feeble, "Why. . . ?" before expiring.

Siward looked down at the broken sailor, emotion drained from his features. Days under the tutelage of Bandares had worked wonders with him.

"Because I can."

Lifetap
(Alpha, Beta, Unlimited, Revised, 4th Edition)

Hassan made his way through the undergrowth and vegetation of the woods with the determination for which the Ashashid were renowned. Black leather gauntlets pushed aside overhanging branches, hard leather riding boots kicked stumps and fallen logs out of the way.

Card Name:	**Lifetap**
Color:	**Blue**
Spell Type:	**Enchantment**
Casting Cost:	**UU**
P/T:	-

Gain 1 life each time any Forest of opponent's becomes tapped.

He stopped for a moment, closed his eyes, and felt the Beast drawing on the power of the woods around him. Hassan allowed himself the luxury of a smile. . .the Beast was as yet unaware that his machinations were being used against him. Long skilled in magicks of guile and deception, the Ashashid were adept at their art. Now, every time Beast tapped the forests for power, Hassan utilized his ***Lifetap****.*

A simple Enchantment costing 2 Blue mana, Lifetap gives its controller 1 life each time a forest belonging to an opponent is tapped.

The practical application of this spell is immediately obvious. While Lifetap is in play, no rational Green Mage will make heavy and extensive use of his or her forests. The fast mana nature of green is immediately rendered less than effective as Lifetap penalizes your opponent for using his resources. This isn't the only reason Lifetap should be a staple spell when facing Green Magi, and even those of other colors as well.

In order to encourage the tapping of Forests, a wide variety of methods can be utilized. With Twiddle or the Icy Manipulator, or the Elder Druid, you can simply take the task upon yourself, tapping your foe's forests to provide you with life. While an easy and effective way to both deny sources of mana and gain life, there are other methods as well. Mana Short, Power Sink and other spells which force the tapping of land while providing other benefits as well all increase the productivity of Lifetap. Using Phantasmal Terrain to create more forests, using Psychic Venom on lands other than Forests, and destroying all lands beyond forests are all ways in which your opponent can be persuaded to provide you with life.

Lifetap can even be used successfully against other land types as well. Simply change the text on Lifetap by means of Magical Hack. If someone is playing Red/Green, bring out two Lifetaps and Hack the text on one to read "Mountain." This can immediately shut down direct damage that targets you, as every mana spent to power a Fireball will provide you with a life as a land is tapped. This can also be a means of surprising an opponent. No Black Mage expects to face Lifetap. . .imagine the look on his or her face when a Hacked Lifetap alters that expectation.

There are drawbacks, however. The value of Lifetap is lessened if a Mana Flare is on the table, since only one-half of the normal number of Forests will need to be tapped. Just as Magical Hack can be used to your benefit, it can be used to your detriment as well. A Blue/Green player can easily Hack the text on Lifetap to read Swamp, rendering it useless. In addition, the color against which Lifetap is most useful also has the most effective means of getting rid of it in Tranquility. Other anti-enchantment cards are just as much of a threat.

Hassan opened his eyes as the presence of the Beast passed over him. Refreshed, strength filling his limbs, he renewed his journey through the ancient wood. Though the Beast was unwittingly supplying him with the tools he would need to face him, it was hardly idle in its own efforts.

Across the ocean, far to the East, the Beast allowed itself a smile.

Magical Hack

(Alpha, Beta, Unlimited, Revised, 4th Edition)

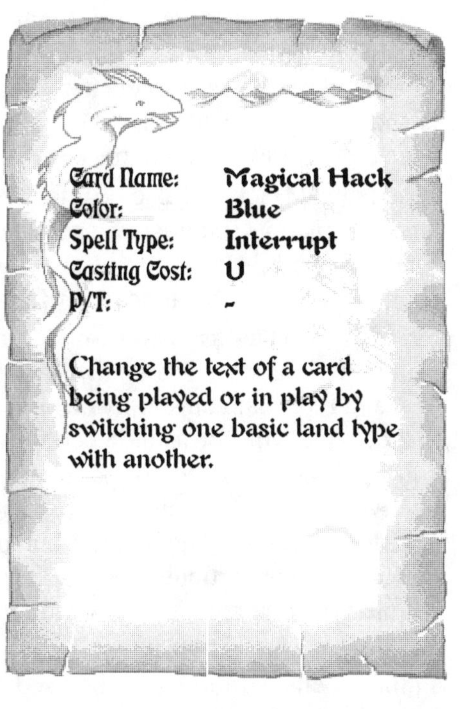

Ariana stood at the door to the laboratory, wrapping herself in a bearskin to ward off the chill. She smiled as El-Hajjaj left the room in disgust, muttering something about fool scholars thinking they are justified in rewriting history.

Within the cluttered laboratory, filled to capacity with arcane apparatus, flywheel-laden devices, and an immense orrery, Canticle poured over a sheaf of papers, frantically jotting notes and retracing mystic symbols. While there were numerous ways of referring to the alteration of the nature of a spell, the more cynical called it a ***Magical Hack****.*

At a cost of 1 Blue mana, Magical Hack may be the most important Interrupt available to a practitioner of Blue. When used, Magical Hack changes the very nature of a spell. The text is altered so that any basic land type may be replaced with another. For instance, any reference to "Plains" becomes a reference to "Forests."

There are two main methods of utilizing Magical Hack, both of which require extensive explanation. The first method is on spells which belong to you, the second method on spells which belong to your opponent. Each method involves variations and intricacies all their own.

When using spells which make reference to land types, it is always a prudent idea to include Magical Hack in your calculations. Using Magical Hack on your Lord of Atlantis, for example, can allow your Merfolk army to Swampwalk rather than Islandwalk, making a Merfolk-based spellbook effective against almost any land type. Spells which provide some sort of walking ability, like Fishliver Oil or War Barge, or spells which deny landwalking, like Undertow, can all be Hacked to affect a land type of your choice.

Used on specific creatures, Magical Hack can be equally effective. Creatures with abilities based on land, such as Gaia's Liege or Seasinger, can be used to greater effect. If your opponent does not use Islands, a Sea Serpent or DanDan can simply be Hacked to a land type which will allow them to attack.

Magical Hack can also be effective when used in conjunction with land destruction spells such as Tsunami, Flashfires, and Acid Rain. The text can be Hacked to allow you to destroy a land type of your choice. As a surprise tactic, this often works wonders.

Magical Hack is also a wonderful way to shut down your opponent's spells as well. If a landwalker is causing you problems, Hack it to a land type that you simply do not possess. When spells are in effect that penalize you for using a certain type of land, Hack it to penalize your opponent instead. A particularly nasty example of this tactic involves using Magical Hack on Thelon's Chant. Hack the text to read Forest, and immediately your opponent will regret playing it. Obviously, this particular use applies only to Black/Blue spellbooks, but the principle remains the same for other colors as well.

Just as Magical Hack can be used effectively with Tsunami and similar spells, so too can it be used to defend against them as well. Hack the text on the cards to destroy your opponent's lands instead of your own, and you're set.

Due to its nature as an Interrupt, the only real effective counter to Magical Hack is a Counterspell or another Magical Hack. Once successfully cast, there is little one can do to alter the effects which have been produced. This makes Magical Hack a potent weapon in any arsenal.

Canticle finished his notations with a flourish and left the laboratory in such a rush that he nearly tripped over the gremlin who was sleeping at the base of the door. He motioned for Ariana to follow and explained as he made his way down the stairs.

"This contest is about far more than usual, with higher stakes than ever. Even so, Bandares remains predictable. And that predictability will prove his downfall. With the loosing of the Beast, his desire to reach Easthold will only increase, allowing us to. . . ."

Canticle stopped dead in his tracks as he entered the study. Slapping a hand to his forehead, dropping his notes, he wished to all the powers that it simply wasn't so, and that the Lord of the Mountain was not standing in the middle of his study.

Mana Short

(Alpha, Beta, Unlimited, Revised, 4th Edition)

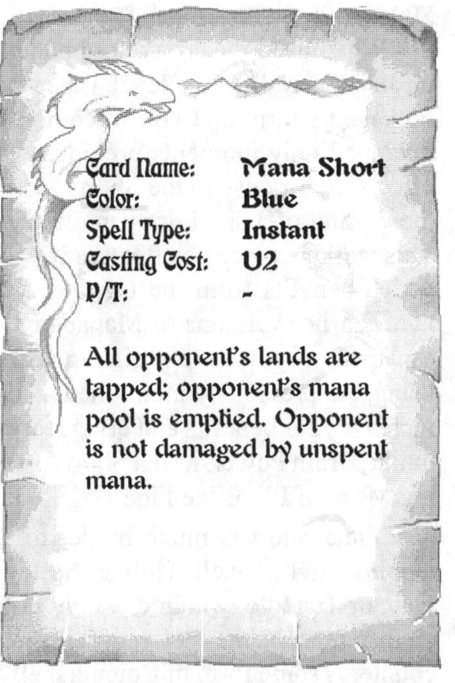
Card Name: Mana Short
Color: Blue
Spell Type: Instant
Casting Cost: U2
P/T: -

All opponent's lands are tapped; opponent's mana pool is emptied. Opponent is not damaged by unspent mana.

The Lord of the Mountain stood in the center of the study, holding a wriggling gremlin up by an ear.

"I believe this belongs to you?"

Canticle simply nodded, unable to come to terms with what was in essence a nightmare made reality. The Lord of the Mountain, here, in his tower.

"Now there's this little matter of a contest that I'd like to bring up with you, one to which I wasn't invited. An oversight, I'm sure, but a serious breach of. . . ."

The Necromancer cut the Lord of the Mountain off with a series of gesticulations and mumbled phrases, frowning as he found himself incapable of casting the spell he so longed to hurl at the Lord.

"Tut tut, don't think I haven't come prepared. Simple matter, really, to avoid all the unpleasantness of a duel with a ***Mana Short****.*

Costing 1 Blue and 2 Colorless, Mana Short is often considered a more widely available alternative to the Time Vault. When this Instant is cast, all of an opponent's lands are tapped, and his or her mana pool is emptied. While unspent mana does not deal damage, the ramifications of this kind of event are obvious.

Used during your own turn, Mana Short can insure that you safely cast any spell that you wish, without fear of having it Pyroblasted or Counterspelled out from under you. In addition, since all of your foe's lands are tapped, any abilities his creatures possess which may require an activation cost are severely reduced in effectiveness. If your opponent has a large number of Drudge Skeletons and Walls of Bone, for example, cast Mana Short after he or she has assigned blockers.

Another excellent way to use Mana Short during your turn is after casting Winter Orb. This effectively denies your opponent an entire turn as he or she attempts to dig out from the effects of the Orb after you've completed your turn.

When used during your opponent's turn, Mana Short is inspiring on an entirely different level. Cast it at the first opportunity during your opponent's turn, and you force him or her to tap the lands he or she untapped only moments previous. While your opponent can use fast effects in response to the Short, and while it cannot be used to prevent the casting of a spell, it is an effective means of limiting his options. This tactic is twice as effective if you have some sort of Enchantment which benefits from the tapping and or untapping of an opponent's land. Earlier versions of Manabarbs can prove to be quite gruesome, especially if you have a Lifetap geared towards the lands he or she is using. As previously mentioned, adding a Winter Orb to the mix will increase your benefits and bring tears to an opponent's eye. In addition, unlike Drain Power, Mana Short forces the tapping of all lands, including Maze of Ith or Ice Floe.

Mana Short is much harder to deal with than other methods of tapping land as well. Unlike the Icy Manipulator, which remains in play, or Twiddle, which can only target one land, Mana Short is both an Instant and a mass effect spell. As an Instant, the only real effective counter is some form of Counterspell, while it covers far more territory than Twiddle. Potent and versatile, Mana Short is a staple in any Permission-based spellbook.

Canticle simply stood there, jaw working furiously as he tried to stammer a response. Ariana, coughing into her hand, slumped into a nearby chair, amazed at the audacity of their visitor.

"Now, since this contest could clearly cause a wide variety of problems for the people who have the misfortune of getting in your way, I've assigned myself as referee. . . ."

Canticle's eyes practically burst from their sockets as he bellowed.

"REFEREE?! I wouldn't assign you the task of boiling water!"

The Lord of the Mountain tapped his chin, tsking all the while. He motioned to the goblin scribe clinging to his robes.

"Disrespect towards an official, extremely unsportsmanlike indeed."

Mind Bomb

(The Dark, 4th Edition)

El-Hajjaj entered the study unseen and unheard, stepping out from behind the bookshelf. He had been examining the contents of the cellar, hoping to find something which would prove useful against the Beast. His unsuccessful search, however, proved fortuitous indeed, for he now found himself standing directly behind the blindingly garish form of the Lord of the Mountain.

"Now look Canticle, enough of this nonsense about the Beast. It's a wonderfully charming myth, but we both know it's a product of your public relations department. . . ."

The Lord of the Mountain was stopped mid-speech as El-Hajjaj tossed out a ***Mind Bomb****.*

Card Name:	Mind Bomb
Color:	Blue
Spell Type:	Sorcery
Casting Cost:	U
P/T:	-

Do 3 damage to each player. Players may discard up to 3 cards. Each discarded card prevents 1 damage from Mind Bomb to that player.

At first, this 1 Blue mana sorcery appears counterproductive. When cast, all players, including the caster, receive 3 damage. For every card a player discards from his or her hand, 1 damage may be prevented. There are subtle and powerful uses to this spell which cannot go ignored.

First of all, Mind Bomb is the ideal way to pull out from under the effects of an early Black Vise. A first or second turn Black Vise can be an annoying and even crippling experience, one which can be alleviated by the casting of Mind Bomb. Not only is the Bomb benefiting you in this situation, it is forcing your opponent to discard cards or take damage.

Apart from this, Mind Bomb has the added benefit of allowing you to choose the cards you discard in order to prevent damage. In a properly constructed spellbook, this can be an incredibly potent weapon. Consider the classic reanimation strategy, which relies on Dance of the Dead, Animate Dead, and creatures which recycle out of the graveyard. Using Mind Bomb on the first turn, you can discard a Sengir Vampire, and Animate it the very next turn. If you have an Ashen Ghoul and Nether Shadow in hand, tossing them into the graveyard by means of a Mind Bomb might be even more productive than casting them from the outset of the duel. In extreme or fortuitous cases, multiple Mind Bombs can be devastating. Casting a Rack on the first Turn and 2 Mind Bombs on the second is simply vicious. So long as you're relying on a reanimation strategy, and have creatures and spells which benefit from the presence of cards in the graveyard, this kind of tactic is almost always to your benefit. Even better, cast Mind Bomb when you have a Circle of Protection: Blue in play. This allows you to avoid both damage and discard while forcing your opposition to make the very same choice.

With the discard strategy, Mind Bomb proves just as effective. With a Rack in play, a late-stage Mind Bomb can provide a truly unpleasant choice to an opponent who has few cards in hand. Either take damage from the Mind Bomb, or discard cards and take damage from the Rack. If your opponent has fewer than three cards in hand, the point is almost moot. It's damage either way. So long as you can afford to discard cards and your opponent cannot, Mind Bomb is a cheap and effective weapon.

When facing Mind Bomb, there are several ways of preventing the worst effects. Simplest of all, obviously, is discarding three cards and taking no damage. If you're in a position where you can afford to do so, fine. However, this is seldom the case. You may choose simply to take the damage and hope for the best, although this can be the shortest route to defeat. Counterspells are effective, as are the classic Red Elemental Blasts. However, beyond making an unpleasant choice, your best bet is a Circle of Protection: Blue.

The Lord of the Mountain staggered under the force of the psychic assault, startled into inactivity. Canticle and Ariana, prepared for the attack on spotting El-Hajjaj's arrival from the cellars, wiped spells from memory and concentrated on getting rid of their most unwelcome guest.

"You have no idea how good this makes me feel," Canticle practically laughed out loud as a softly glowing disk descended over the Lord of the Mountain. It slowly absorbed him, and once it hit the floor, all trace of the flamboyant mage had disappeared. The goblin scribe, astounded at the display, dropped his quill pen and writing tablet, launching his arms into the air.

"Oh bother. . . ."

*Ariana snapped her fingers, and a loud *POP* echoed in the study. The goblin disappeared, transported to the side of his master.*

"Now, I do believe we've got more important things to concentrate on."

Phantasmal Terrain

(Alpha, Beta, Unlimited, Revised, 4th Edition)

"Canticle's sense of humor leaves a great deal to be desired. . . ."

The Lord of the Mountain muttered as he paced the edge of the cliff, frost-rimed winds filling the folds and creases of his multicolored robes, causing them to billow magnificently. His goblin scribe huddled behind him for warmth. Canticle and Ariana had transported the two of them to the tallest mountain in the chain which ringed the Mourning Lands.

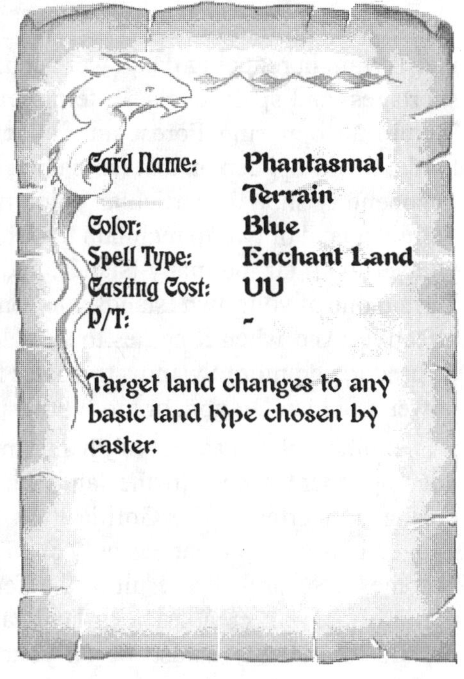

The Lord of the Mountain sniffed the air and snorted. Poking at the cliff wall, he muttered darkly to himself.

"Hmph, just as I thought, ***Phantasmal Terrain****."*

When this 2 Blue mana Enchant Land is cast, a target land of your choice is altered in nature, becoming a basic land type of your choice. Obviously a valuable addition to the arsenal of an accomplished illusionist, Phantasmal Terrain proves its worth in a wide range of situations.

The simplest and perhaps most devastating use of this spell is when it is used to destroy specialty lands. The Library of Alexandria, the Diamond Valley and Oasis can be rendered all but useless through the use of Phantasmal Terrain. To increase the lethality of this application, use landwalkers of a particular type. For example, if you use Phantasmal Terrain to turn the Library of Alexandria into a Swamp, have a Bog Wraith handy to take advantage of the situation. Multilands can be destroyed in this manner as well: turn an Underground River into a Plains, and your opponent will not be at all amused.

This illustrates another common use for Phantasmal Terrain: the ability to provide creatures and landwalkers with the tools of their trade. If an opponent uses nothing but Mountains, use the Terrain to create an Island, allowing you to use DanDan and the Sea Serpent. If you have a control deck and want to maximize its effectiveness, use Phantasmal Terrain to allow your Seasinger access to her powers.

Slightly more obscure, yet no less effective, is the use of Phantasmal Terrain in reducing the power and impact of upkeep effects, mana shortages, and spell levels. In terms of upkeep, you can Phantasmal Terrain an opposing Forest into something else entirely, making it harder to pay upkeep on that rampaging Force of Nature. Or when your opponent is short a particular color of mana, you can Phantasmal Terrain a land or two to maintain that shortage. Alternately, if you find yourself with far too many Islands, and too few Swamps, Phantasmal Terrain one of your own Islands into something which will prove more effective. And when it comes to spell levels, Phantasmal Terrain can be used to add more Swamps to power Drain Life, more Mountains to power a Shivan Dragon, or more Forests to power Gaia's Liege.

Another related aspect of Phantasmal Terrain is its use in denying your opponent access to the lands he needs or requires for certain creatures or effects. The Gorilla Pack can be quickly and easily destroyed if your opponent has only one Forest in play. When that forest becomes a Swamp as a result of the Terrain, the Pack is destroyed. If you are facing a creature with landwalking, simply use Phantasmal Terrain to alter the landscape on your side, preventing the creature from breaking through.

Subject to the usual dangers that face Enchantments, Phantasmal Terrain also suffers from the fact that it can be overridden by numerous other effects. Gaia's Liege can create forests on a whim, Phantasmal Terrain may alter the landscape yet again, while Illusionary Terrain can alter lands in one fell swoop. Care must be taken when applying this spell, as powerful as it may be.

The Lord of the Mountain looked down at his scribe, smirking triumphantly.

"This will be simple enough."

Snapping his fingers, the Lord dispelled the magicks which had led them to believe they were trapped atop a snow encrusted peak. Within moments, they were mired in the thick, black sludge of the Mourning Lands, waist-deep in the furthest reaches of the Marsh.

The slowly sinking mage simply shook his head, admonishing himself.

"I knew I recognized that smell from somewhere. . . ."

Power Leak

(Alpha, Beta, Unlimited, Revised, 4th Edition)

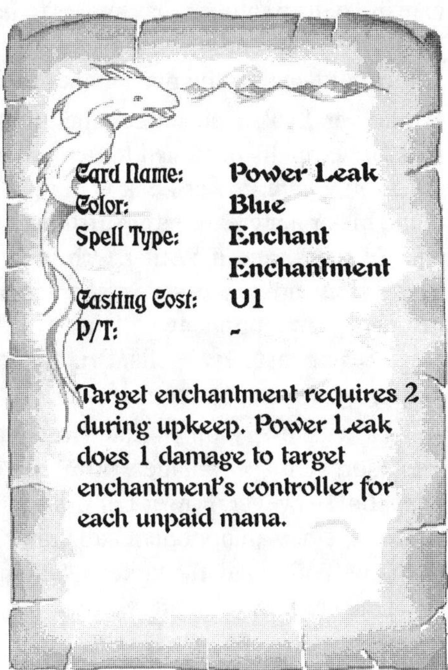

As the three companions made their way through the Mourning Lands, an oppressive weight seemed to fill the very air around them. With every passing moment, Bandares drew closer to his goal, the Beast gained in awareness, and Torwynn came one step closer to cataclysm.

Canticle stumbled over a partially submerged stump, landing face-first in the mire. A pair of gremlins leapt from behind cover, striking defensive postures before their fallen master. It was a few moments before the Necromancer could regain his footing. He seemed pale and wan, far more so than usual. Ariana looked at him with concern, though he brushed her hand aside.

"There is no time—the enchantments which ring my tower have been tainted by a ***Power Leak****."*

An enchantment costing 1 Blue and 1 Colorless, this spell targets any other enchantment in play. The target enchantment now costs 2 mana during the upkeep of its controller's phase. If this mana is not paid, Power Leak does 1 damage to him or her for each mana which is unpaid.

One thing which this Enchantment does extremely well is deny mana to your opponent. Rather than utilizing 2 mana in the casting of a spell or the summoning of a creature, it will often go to the prevention of damage and maintenance of the enchantment. This spell is particularly effective against White, which possesses a wide variety of beneficial enchantments. Circles of Protection usually allow the White Mage to avoid a great deal of unnecessary damage, but having them enchanted with Power Leak immediately becomes a costly venture. A Circle of Protection: Blue can still be used to avoid the damage at a cost of 1 mana rather than 2, but it is still an expense which your opponent will not appreciate. Power Leak is also an excellent way of causing detrimental enchantments to backfire on their controller. Paralyze, Psychic Venom, Phantasmal Terrain and Seizures are all excellent candidates for the placement of a Power Leak.

Power Leak reaches new heights of horror when it is combined with other spells designed to deny mana to your opponent. Imagine a situation where Power Leak is in play against an opponent's Enchantment, his or her creatures are afflicted with Errant Minion, Mind Whip, and Seizures, and a Winter Orb is in play. Your opponent must pay tremendous upkeep costs or take damage, and while the Winter Orb is in play, your opponent will have little to no time to summon new creatures or cast new spells. Brutal and efficient, this combination can quickly grind an opponent under.

As with every other Enchantment, Power Leak suffers from the same sort of disadvantages, primarily a susceptibility to a wide range of spells. However, Power Leak is somewhat more self preservative in nature. . .since an opponent can either pay upkeep or take damage, he or she will often pay the upkeep, leaving less available mana for things like Disenchant and Tranquility.

Canticle staggered forward, with the assistance of El-Hajjaj and Ariana. Though he valued his tower and all it contained, their mission was far more important.

Psychic Venom

(Alpha, Beta, Unlimited, Revised, 4th Edition)

Chained to the trunk of a blackened, scorched oak, he hardly seems human. Wild streaks of white hair splay out in all directions from his face, matted with twigs, mud, drool and blood. His pale blue eyes bulge with madness, and his lithe frame twists and contorts with rage and fury. A tattered loin cloth is his only clothing, given to him ages ago by the marsh goblins, who regard him as a deity. In truth, he is a fallen archmage, imprisoned here centuries ago. His immense power was his downfall, for now whenever he attempts to tap the lands around him, he falls prey to ***Psychic Venom****.*

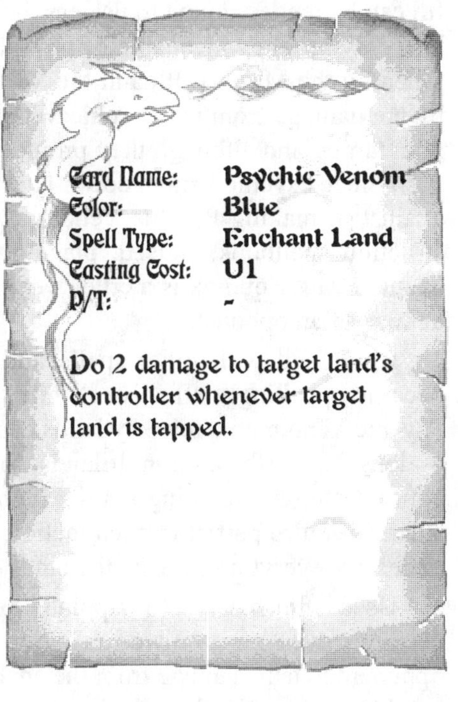

A simple enough spell, which enchants any single target land, Psychic Venom costs a mere 1 Blue and 1 Colorless to bring into play. Whenever the land which this spell enchants is tapped, for whatever reason, Psychic Venom inflicts 2 points of damage on the controller of that land.

There are numerous applications for this spell, in a variety of circumstances. One of the more mundane, yet effective, uses for Psychic Venom is to place it on lands which your opponent values highly. For example, if a foe is using both forests and mountains, yet only has forests in play, it would be prudent to place Psychic Venom on the first Mountain which he or she plays. Early in the duel, if an opponent is short of mana, Psychic Venom can give an effective and early edge. Combined with the Black Vise, a second turn Psychic Venom can be a painful experience.

However, the most popular use of Psychic Venom is probably the most dangerous to an opponent: using it to shut down specialty lands. There are numerous lands which provide benefits beyond mana, or instead of mana, and it is these which are most vulnerable to enchantment. The Library of Alexandria, the Diamond Valley and the Maze of Ith can be rendered next to useless through the use of Psychic Venom. Not only are they incapable of providing mana, but the benefits provided by the Maze of Ith and the Valley are almost instantly negated by the damage from the Psychic Venom. Multilands are another common target, and although they provide mana, it won't come without a cost. Since Psychic Venom doesn't destroy land, Equinox is ineffective against it, making Psychic Venom a potential addition to a land destruction spellbook. Indeed, placing Psychic Venom on a land enchanted with Equinox is a cruel, yet effective way of speeding up the demise of an opponent.

Combined with other spells and artifacts, Psychic Venom can become appallingly effective. While the Winter Orb is in play, using Psychic Venom on a few key lands can severely restrict an opponent's options. Using them on multilands, for example, forces him or her to concentrate on untapping lands which they would not normally consider. If you're partial to such tactics, you could use land destruction to destroy everything except the lands enchanted with Psychic Venom.

Used with the Icy Manipulator or Elder Druid, Psychic Venom becomes even more powerful. Now, you are capable of forcing an opponent to take damage from the enchanted land, when normally you would have to wait. Twiddle, Power Sink, Mana Short can also be used to accomplish this goal, although they are a little more limited in this respect, as they can only be used once. Nonetheless, forcing an opponent to take damage is not something one should pass up. Against a Green Mage, an amusing combination involves Psychic Venom and Lifetap. Using Psychic Venom on any lands which are not forests, one can force an opponent to use lands which will provide you with life. While not the most practical or effective use, it can be worth the time and effort involved.

Psychic Venom, however, is not without its drawbacks. If an opponent has sources of mana other than those provided by land, he or she can avoid the worst of Psychic Venom. In addition, since it is highly unlikely that there will ever be four Psychic Venoms out at once; the more land that is in play, the less effective it becomes. As an enchantment, it is also highly susceptible to a large number of spells which can quickly terminate its usefulness. Nevertheless, it can be a valuable enchantment in a wide variety of situations.

Once again, the old man focused his attention on the tower in the distance, eyes burning with hatred. His jailer had long ago turned to dust, yet still he remained trapped, his desire for revenge fueling his determination to escape. Only when the tower was destroyed would he truly be free to walk Torwynn again. Only then would he know peace.

Green Spells

Birds of Paradise

(Alpha, Beta, Unlimited, Revised, 4th Edition)

It took Siward a few moments to notice the excitement on the foredeck. Occupied in thought, it took him time to notice much of anything, beyond the ever expanding nature of his powers. It wouldn't be long before he would be able to challenge Bandares himself, he was sure of it. He shook his head to clear away such thoughts.

"What is it?"

One of the crew pointed to a pair of birds which were circling around the prow of the ship. Their brilliant plumage danced under the light of the sun, and they flew elaborate patterns in the air around them.

"Easthold must be near. . . ."

To Siward, it was obvious. While they were considered a scavenging nuisance on the island kingdom of Easthold, the rest of Torwynn referred to them as ***Birds of Paradise****.*

Card Name:	**Birds of Paradise**
Color:	**Green**
Spell Type:	**Summon Creature**
Casting Cost:	**G**
P/T:	**0/1**

Flying. T: Add one mana of any color to your mana pool.

At a cost of 1 Green mana, these 0/1 Flyers are often referred to as Manabirds. This is due to their special ability. The Birds of Paradise may be tapped to add one mana of any color to your mana pool, an ability which has proven valuable time and again.

Due to their low cost, Birds of Paradise are often used as sources of cheap, fast mana. First-turn Manabirds usually allow a Mage to access three mana on the second turn, one of which can be the color of his or her choice from the Birds. This not only effectively speeds up the spellbook, but also provides more flexibility. Spells which require more than one Green mana in their casting cost, for example, can be cast even if there is only one forest in play. Alternately, you can include spells of a specific color without including the lands of that color.

If you are playing a straight Green spellbook, Manabirds, Fire-sprites and Tinder Walls can provide you with the ability to surprise your opponent at inopportune moments. With these creatures as sources of Red mana, consider including Lightning Bolt, Fireball, and Disintegrate to increase the damage potential. Alternately, using items like the Celestial Prism in conjunction with the Mana Birds, you could bring spells like Armageddon into play, a completely unexpected ploy from a spellbook which appears to rely exclusively on Green.

The Birds of Paradise also benefit from the fact that they are a non-land source of mana. If you are playing with the Winter Orb, for example, the Mana Birds are an excellent source of additional power for your spells. Add Instill Energy, and you can tap the Birds twice in a single turn to provide mana of your choice. Combined with the effects of Armageddon, this can be a decisive advantage. One of the deadliest combinations with the Birds of Paradise is the Stasis lock. While Stasis is in play, and if the Birds of Paradise have had Instill Energy put on them, you can secure yourself a victory in short order.

The Birds of Paradise, however, are far from ideal. At 0/1, they are vulnerable to a wide variety of magicks. In addition, they aren't very effective attackers or blockers, lacking the power and toughness required if you wanted to use them as backup. For their cost, however, they are an effective and valuable tool.

The birds wheeled and circled a few moments more, until the ship's cook tossed the scraps and remnants from the morning meal out the hatch. They then descended with a decidedly undignified series of caws to the surface waters, cheerfully consuming the morsels.

Siward was already on his way to the Captain's cabin. Easthold was fast approaching.

Channel

(Alpha, Beta, Unlimited, Revised, 4th Edition)

Card Name: Channel
Color: Green
Spell Type: Sorcery
Casting Cost: GG
P/T: -

Add 1 colorless mana to your pool for each life point you sacrifice.

"I can do nothing for these people. . . ."

Canticle swept his arm in a wide arc, encompassing the entire port district. Ash and embers fell at his feet, descending from the wretched black cloud which hung over Blacksand. Most of the port district was in flames, streets choked with rubble, burning timber, and desperate citizens. Somewhere in the distance, a child wailed for its mother. Ariana cringed at the sound, coughing into her arm as pillars of smoke drifted in on the winds.

"We have to find a ship, and quickly." Canticle stopped short as they turned into a blind alley. Shattered stonework, charred beams and an overturned cart blocked their passage. The Necromancer wasted little time, drawing on his own life force by means of a ***Channel****.*

At a cost of 2 Green mana, this Sorcery is a spell of hidden powers. After it has been cast, and until the end of your turn, you may add Colorless mana to your pool at a cost of 1 life per mana.

Some of the more time-honored methods of using Channel are also some of the deadliest. This includes a wide variety of methods which can secure victory almost before the duel has begun. Using a Black Lotus and Channel on the first turn, for example, you can launch a Fireball sufficient in size to roast your opponent. For those without access to the Lotus, an effective alternative exists in the Orcish Lumberjacks. On the first turn, summon the Lumberjacks. Next turn, play a Forest. Tap the Lumberjacks to sacrifice the Forest, providing you with 3 green mana. Tapping the Forest before sacrificing it is perfectly legal as well and only adds to the size of the forthcoming spell. Using Channel, the Mountain, and the leftover Green mana, cast a 20-point Fireball. This guarantees a kill so long as your opponent doesn't surprise you with a Blue Elemental Blast. Black has an equally appalling method of dealing damage, although it may take a little longer to set up. If the Initiates of the Ebon Hand are in play, Channel 19 life into 19 mana, funneling it through the Initiates to create 19 Black mana. Then cast Drain Life on your opposition. The end result is a gain in life sufficient to replace what was lost through Channel, and a dead opponent.

Other combinations, while less spectacular to witness, are no less effective. If you have a Black Vise in play, use Channel to Braingeyser a large number of cards into your opponent's hand. The Vise deals a large amount of damage to your opponent in turn, and he or she will be forced to discard several by the end of the turn. Alternately, if you possess a Library of Leng and an Ivory Tower, Braingeyser yourself for several cards. The loss of life will be more than compensated by the effects of the Ivory Tower over time.

Consider the application of Channel in conjunction with the Mirror Universe. In this case, Channel 19 of your life into a Stream of Life, cast upon your opponent. While this should only be done when you can assure that you won't take damage during your opponent's turn, it is nevertheless a risky maneuver. However, you can then activate Mirror Universe, switching life totals.

Finally, witness the effectiveness of Channel in an artifact-laden spellbook. Two forests on the second turn, and you can Channel as much life as you desire into the casting of Artifacts and Artifact Creatures. Channeling 8 life, for example, can summon 2 Juggernauts on the second turn, a force your opponent will be hard-pressed to stop.

Channel is, however, dangerous. Counterspells and Elemental Blasts can be used to counter those spells which life was channeled into casting, and there is no way to recover the lost life. Care must be exercised when using a potent weapon like Channel, lest it backfire.

A pillar of pure concussive force erupted from Canticle's outstretched arms, blasting a path through the debris and rubble. The exertion of casting the spell drained the Necromancer, and he stumbled against a nearby wall. El-Hajjaj and Ariana both took an arm, supporting him on their shoulders. Struggling beneath his weight, they made their way through the breach and towards the docks beyond.

In the chaos and confusion, they never noticed the black-clad form that followed close behind.

Crumble

(Antiquities, Revised, 4th Edition)

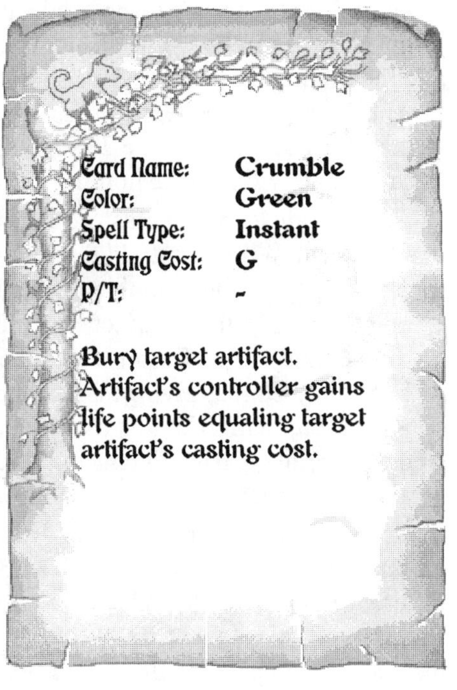

The Lord of the Mountain stood atop a granite outcropping, looking out to sea with a triumphant smirk. For all their posturing and grandiose casting of spells, Canticle and Bandares were leagues away, while here he was, at their final destination. He glanced over his shoulder at the old man who had brought both him and his assistant here, tossing a cheerful little wave. The old man simply grunted and continued rocking back and forth on his heels. The Lord of the Mountain rubbed his hands together and looked down at his goblin scribe. The spindly little creature brought his immense quill to bear and began to take notes.

"Well, here we are. Now this," he said, tapping the side of an unremarkable stone pillar, "Is the object of their little quest. One wants to control it, the other wants to protect it."

The Lord of the Mountain chuckled to himself.

"Now let's see what happens when we destroy it. . . ."

Placing his hands on the side of the pillar, the Lord of the Mountain called to mind the rituals necessary for ***Crumble****.*

First developed during the Brothers War as a means of dealing with the twisted artifacts so prevalent in that time, this Sorcery costs 1

Green mana to cast. It buries a target artifact and gives the controller of that artifact life equal to the casting cost of the buried artifact.

One of the most obvious uses for this spell is against the numerous 0 casting cost artifacts which are in existence. Those who rely too much on the power of the Moxen may find their artifacts turning to dust before their eyes, and they won't be receiving life as compensation. Other popular artifacts are in equal danger. For those who seek to protect themselves against Red magicks, the Dark Sphere has proven a boon. . .one which can be eradicated by Crumble, which is then followed by a Fireball. The Ornithopter is a popular creature which is all too vulnerable to this spell. The Zuran Orb, which is truly a vexing piece of work, can be removed as a concern as well. The Fountain of Youth, Tormod's Crypt, the Jewelled Amulet. . .all are vulnerable to Crumble and will provide nothing to their controller upon destruction.

Even against artifact creatures of a more malevolent bent, Crumble can be useful. While most Magi hesitate to give their opponent any sort of advantage, casting Crumble on a creature may be the fastest way to be rid of it. In addition, artifact creatures destroyed in this manner may not regenerate. Thus, Crumble may be the most effective way to deal with the Clay Statue, Living Wall or the Diabolic Machine. While your opponent may gain life, it is usually better than you losing your own. And if Crumble is used to take out a key blocker, the temporary boost of life to an opponent is of little concern.

Using Crumble on your own artifacts may at first seem counterproductive, but it can provide quick boosts which may prove to be the difference between life and death. While no one can dispute the value of a Mana Battery, the 4 life it can provide may be worth far more than the mana it can provide. In one particular duel, a Green Mana Battery was drained to provide fuel for a Stream of Life, and then Crumble was cast on the Battery to add that much more. In a situation like this, the infusion of life could conceivably be used to power a Channel.

Such a tactic can also save you a great deal of trouble when one of your own artifacts has been rendered useless or inert through spells and artifacts such as Titania's Song, Artifact Possession, or any other deleterious magick.

Destroying your own Artifacts to gain life becomes even more appealing in a Green/White spellbook. With Enduring Renewal in play, one could sacrifice a high casting cost Artifact Creature, only to have it return to your hand after being buried. You would still gain the life from the artifact, and it would still be available for use. Used on a creature like the Colossus of Sardia, such a ploy could prove truly devastating. The existence of spells and creatures such as Reconstruction and the Argivian Archaeologist make such a ploy far more palatable, since one can be reasonably assured of retrieving the destroyed artifact. Combined with the effects of Soul Net and the Tablet of Epityr, the destruction of something like a Su-Chi or Onulet can provide far more than its continued existence.

Crumble does have its drawbacks. Unlike other anti-artifact spells, it cannot be used during your opponent's turn. In addition to this, it does provide an opponent with a boost to life with the destruction of an artifact. The more powerful and valuable the device, the more life is received, as a general rule. In addition, against Mox, Crumble cannot prevent an opponent from tapping it for mana before it is destroyed. None of this, however, relegates it to the realm of the useless and mundane. In any Green spellbook which expects to face artifacts, Crumble can be a valuable addition.

As the pillar dissolved into powder, a hollow, barren laugh echoed across the mountains of Easthold. In a matter of moments, still air was whipping across the island with the force of a gale, while storm clouds gathered with unnatural speed. Freed of its final bond, the Beast was free to do as it wished.

The Lord of the Mountain held on to the edges of his robe, staring up into a darkening sky.

"Make a note of this. Next time, we conduct a little more research."

Ghazban Ogre
(Arabian Nights, Chronicles)

"Shhhh, my pet. . . ."

The Queen of Cameshbaan stood at the prow of her barque, watching as an incredible hole opened in the skies above Easthold. One hand on a leather leash, the other stroking the scaled forehead of her companion, she shook her head in annoyance. The creature at her side let out another plaintive wail.

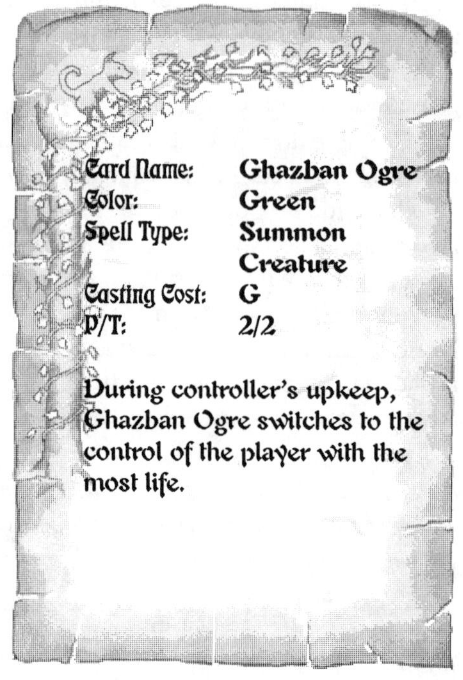

"Yes, yes, I know. . .rather foolish indeed. Now we're simply going to have to let those two have their way with the Beast until we can figure something else out."

Tossing back her head, her braided ebony locks flying in all directions with the motion, she laughed lightly.

"Ah well. . .it will make things all the more interesting."

Turning once again to her scaly companion, she used one of her long nails to gently scratch the chin of the ***Ghazban Ogre****.*

At a cost of 1 Green mana, the 2/2 Ghazban Ogre seems to be the ideal investment. And it would be were it not for the fact that during its current controller's upkeep, the player with the highest life total takes control of the Ogre.

While it may at first seem to be a noxious detriment, there are a variety of ways to maintain control of the Ogre. If played immediately on the first turn and thrown into the attack, there is little reason for you to fear losing control of the beast. If you have the combination of Library of Leng and Ivory Tower on your side, you should be able to manage a comfortable life point lead for the duration of the duel, with the Ghazban Ogre knocking the first few life points off your opponent.

A favorite method of using the Ogre is casting it on the first turn, and then using Giant Growth on it during the second turn attack. Nine times out of ten, it makes for a quick 5 points of damage on the second turn, something which your opponent will seldom recover from. Using Unstable Mutation is another option, which also conveniently destroys the Ogre later in the duel. Essence Flare is probably ideal, as it slowly kills the Ogre while maintaining its increased power. The Ogre is best used as a fast, expendable shock troop.

Of course, in the later stages of a duel, the Ghazban Ogre should never be summoned forth unless you have a comfortable lead in life points, usually around five or more. One method of assuring control over the Ogre is to summon it immediately after casting Stream of Life or similar magicks.

What do you do when you lose control of the Ogre? There are a variety of methods Magi use to deal with such a situation. Unsummon and Word of Undoing are two of the more popular methods, since they allow you to make use of the Ogre at a later point in time. Possession of a Circle of Protection: Green simply allows you to ignore the Ogre until such a time as you are able to retake control. Another method involves the use of the Tabernacle of Pendrell Vale. When you feel control of the Ogre slipping away, simply refuse to pay the upkeep that the Tabernacle requires, killing the beast. Sacrificing the Ogre to the Fallen Angel, the Lord of the Pit or even Life Chisel is another option if the fortunes of the duel turn against you and the risk of losing control is too great. Another, more creative way of dealing with this damage is to use Wanderlust on it while you have a Circle of Protection: Green in play. If the Ogre ever comes under the control of your opponent, it's immediately a problem.

While the Ogre may at first appear to be a bad investment, keep the above in mind. You may find that the Ogre is one of the most effective creatures you can summon early in the duel.

"Patience, sweetness, patience," cooed the Queen, as she continued to scratch the Ogre beneath its chin, "We'll be there soon enough."

Looking out towards Easthold yet again, she smiled.

"Patience is, after all, a virtue."

Giant Growth

(Alpha, Beta, Unlimited, Revised, 4th Edition, Ice Age)

"This isn't going to work. . . ."

Canticle spat over the side of the boat, slamming his fists down against the rail in frustration. Ariana struggled to maintain her footing on the rolling deck, while El-Hajjaj attempted without success to loosen the tarred rope which moored the vessel. All the while, a hail of ash and embers descended around them as the port quarter of Blacksand continued to die.

"Enough! We're wasting time!"

Canticle muttered a phrase and passed his hand through the air, gesturing towards El-Hajjaj. The Tarkaan's robes seemed to grow larger before their eyes, his features inflating. Muscles rippled as he tore the mooring ring free from the dock, his entire frame enhanced by ***Giant Growth****.*

Card Name:	**Giant Growth**
Color:	**Green**
Spell Type:	**Instant**
Casting Cost:	**G**
P/T:	-

Target creature gains +3/+3 until end of turn.

At a cost of 1 Green mana, this Instant is arguably one of the most useful creature enhancements available. When cast, the target creature gains +3/+3 until the end of the turn.

Although not permanent, Giant Growth is by no means at a disadvantage to Enchantments. Indeed, it possesses an element of surprise not available with other spells. In an attack situation, this means that you can wait until an opponent has declared his blocking creatures, and then cast Giant Growth. In a situation where a Sengir Vampire is being blocked by a Serra Angel, this means the difference between losing an attacker and gaining a stronger creature while taking out the defense. In some situations, your opponent may not even block a simple 1/1 creature, opting instead to block bigger threats. Placing a Giant Growth on one of those unblocked creatures means a total of 4 damage.

On the opposite side of things, after an opponent has declared an attack, you can block his other Serra Angel with something like the Bird Maiden. Cast Giant Growth on the Bird Maiden, and you can kill the Serra without losing your defender.

Giant Growth is also an excellent companion with special abilities like Banding and Trample. War Mammoths are fearsome in their own right, but with a Giant Growth become that much more of a threat. Since additional damage carries over, a Giant Growth not only allows them to survive being blocked by a 3/3 creature, but also allows you to deal the added damage to your opponent. In the case where you're using a Band, Giant Growth allows you to allocate 3 more damage while absorbing that much more as well.

Giant Growth can even prove worthwhile on your opponents' creatures under certain circumstances. Casting it on a beast which has been Creature Bonded, for example, allows you to deal extra damage when you destroy the creature. Giant Growth is a multi-purpose spell with a great deal of flexibility, something which every Green Mage should take into consideration.

El-Hajjaj barely managed the leap onto the small craft as it slipped away from the dock. Moments after his spectacular display of strength, his form began to recede in size, his frame returning to its proper proportions. The temporary nature of the spell, however, had been enough.

Ariana took the tiller of the small craft, the Necromancer directing three small gremlins in trimming the sails. Two of them got into a shoving match over a rope, and ended up dangling from it by their feet, still trading punches.

In all the confusion, Hassan was able to slip over the rail and disappear below deck.

Giant Spider

(Alpha, Beta, Unlimited, Revised, 4th Edition)

The Lord of the Mountain scrambled down the trail in as dignified a manner as the situation would allow. The old man had disappeared, swallowed up in some interdimensional vortex which had no doubt led him to safety, leaving him to fend for himself. A few yards ahead of him, quill still in hand, his goblin assistant was careening into the woods which dotted the slopes of the mountain.

Card Name:	**Giant Spider**
Color:	**Green**
Spell Type:	**Summon Creature**
Casting Cost:	**G3**
P/T:	**2/4**

Doesn't fly, but it can block flying creatures.

"I say! Watch out for the. . ."

SPROING

It was too late. The Lord of the Mountain carefully made his way over to his assistant, who was suspended in a sticky morass of webs which had been stretched across the trail. The goblin had been caught in the motion of running, one arm raised high, the other at his side, with his legs splayed in a ridiculous manner.

*"Dear me, I do believe this belongs to a **Giant Spider**."*

Costing 1 Green and 3 Colorless to Summon, the 2/4 Giant Spider, while not a flying creature itself, is capable of blocking those creatures which possess flying.

The Spider is a valuable addition to any spellbook which lacks an effective method of dealing with Flying Creatures. Green, which lacks a large number of flyers itself, can't help but benefit from the presence of a Giant Spider. Its casting cost also allows it to enter play early in the duel, often as soon as the third turn.

Used in conjunction with a surprise Giant Growth, the Giant Spider can defend its controller against some of the more deadly flyers, including the Sengir Vampire and Dragon Whelp. Adding a Venom to the mixture provides you with a defender that is capable of instantly destroying any single creature it blocks, be it earthbound or flying. The Giant Spider can be an ideal way to hold off an attacker until something like Hurricane can be brought to bear. Note that since the Spider itself does not fly, Hurricane will not touch it, yet it still provides you with a measure of security against future flying attacks.

The Giant Spider is also relatively safe against one of the more popular methods of creature control, Lightning Bolt. The toughness level of the Spider practically requires a spell like Fissure or Terror to deal with, providing you with an added measure of security. It should be emphasized that the urge to use the Giant Spider on the attack should be resisted at all costs. While an opponent may not appear to possess flying creatures, spells such as Flight and Jump can change that in an instant. And against such spells, a tapped Giant Spider is of little use. Common sense dictates that the Giant Spider be utilized on the defensive, allowing other creatures to participate in the attack.

The Lord of the Mountain poked at the strands with a stick, muttering to himself as he let go. The stick remained in place, fastened securely to the webs. The goblin let loose with a high-pitched wail, startling his flamboyant master out of his thoughts.

"Oh dear. . ."

Mandibles dripping with ichor, an immense spider was gingerly poking the goblin with its forelegs, four pairs of eyes watching the tiny creature's struggles in fascination. The Lord of the Mountain stepped back, realizing that there was only one real option.

"Duck. . ."

The goblin did its best to twist out of the way as his master launched a flaming bolt of fire directly at the Spider. Impacting with a sizzle, the hairy arachnid shuddered, convulsed, and fell to the earth, legs curling in death. Its death throes, however, ignited the web. . . .

Hurricane

(Alpha, Beta, Unlimited, Revised, 4th Edition, Ice Age)

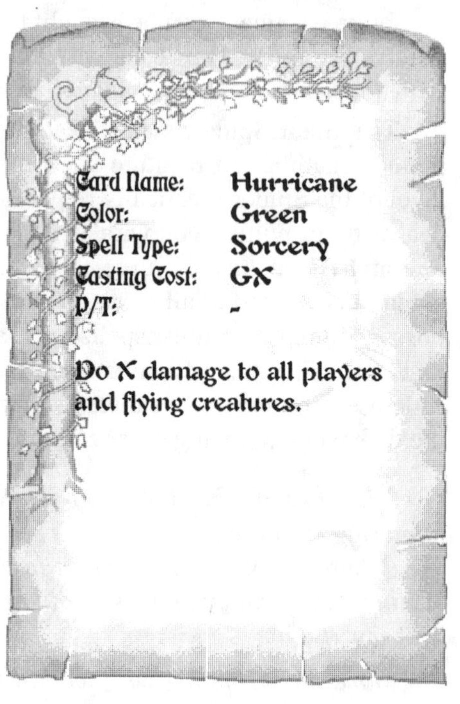

The tiny boat nearly capsized as it struck yet another unnatural wave, tossing it directly through the crest of an oncoming wall of water. Canticle was doused clear through, holding on to the mast as a trio of soggy gremlins worked feverishly to secure a loose sail. Ariana had tied herself to the tiller, the only manner in which she could maintain a grip, while El-Hajjaj tried to make his way towards the hold, where bailing would surely be needed.

*As the three continued on course for Easthold and the dark wall of cloud which seemed to surround the island kingdom, they found themselves in the midst of an unnatural **Hurricane**.*

A Sorcery costing 1 Green and X amount of Colorless mana, this spell deals X damage to all players and flying creatures. Devastating, the true potential of this spell is worse than many realize.

When attempting to deal with Flying creatures, Hurricane is often used as a method of last resort, due to the damage it inflicts on the caster. This damage is easily minimized, or prevented altogether, through the use of Enchantments such as Circle of Protection: Green, or life-providing spells like Stream of Life, Healing Salve and Alabaster Potion. When used in combination with such magicks, Hurricane doubles in effectiveness, taking out a wide variety of flying creatures and at the same time dealing damage to your foe.

There are other ways to increase the effectiveness of Hurricane. Before casting it, use the Radjan Spirit to remove Flying ability from any of your creatures which you want to save from destruction. At the same time, use spells like Jump and Arnjlot's Ascent, or artifacts such as the Flying Carpet, to give opposing creatures Flying. Then cast a 4 or 5 point Hurricane. The resulting carnage usually provides you with a clear avenue of approach from the air, courtesy of the beast you saved from destruction with the Radjan Spirit.

Even if your opponent doesn't utilize Flying creatures, Hurricane can still be a valuable asset. Currently, it remains one of the only direct damage spells available to Green, and used this way may provide a nasty surprise for your opponent. So long as you possess more life than your opponent, a pumped-up Hurricane can end the game. Ideally, you cast Hurricane with a Reverse Damage in hand. Ultimately, Hurricane may prove to be the spell which decides a duel, and in a worst-case scenario, you could use it to turn a defeat into a draw.

El-Hajjaj barely had time to shout a warning before a mountainous wave crashed down upon the vessel, washing gremlins against the rails and sending the Necromancer sprawling on deck. Ariana hacked up gouts of water as she struggled for breath, her grip on the tiller loosed. It was a few moments before the three realized that the vessel was no longer tossing them about, and that the gale force winds were now no more than a whisper.

As they looked out over an ocean as still as a sheet of glass, a sense of unease fell over them all. On the horizon, Easthold sat, a mountainous green line. And above the island, it appeared as if a hole had been torn in the heavens.

Kudzu

(Alpha, Beta, Unlimited, Revised)

"Just remain calm, I'll figure something out."

The Lord of the Mountain stood before the blazing web which contained his goblin scribe, tapping his chin in thought. Things weren't exactly working out as planned. The goblin squealed and fell to the earth as the strands which contained him caught fire and snapped under the strain. The tiny little beast, jerkin smouldering, danced about trying to extinguish his boots, ultimately slamming into a tree.

"Good help is just so hard to find these days. . . ."

The Lord of the Mountain attempted to move, but found his legs securely locked in place by clinging vines of ***Kudzu****.*

Card Name:	**Kudzu**
Color:	**Green**
Spell Type:	**Enchant Land**
Casting Cost:	**GG1**
P/T:	**-**

When target land is tapped, it is destroyed. Unless that was the last land in play, the player that just lost a land to Kudzu must place it on any other land in play. Kudzu is discarded when all lands in play are discarded.

At a cost of 2 Green mana and 1 Colorless, this land Enchantment is often overlooked. If the target land is tapped, the controller of that land moves Kudzu onto a target land of his or her choice, and the original target land is destroyed. If Kudzu has no target lands to move to, it is destroyed.

The obvious question with Kudzu is why. Why would anyone wish to cast a spell with such a chaotic nature? However, Kudzu does have its applications, especially when used to amplify a Land Destruction spellbook. After all, when you are using Psychic Venom, Cursed Land and Stone Rain to shut down mana production, an opponent will be extremely loathe to tap land Enchanted by Kudzu, even if he or she knows that it can then be placed on one of your lands.

It is in this respect that the usefulness of Kudzu exerts itself. If your opponent is dropping nasty Enchantments on your lands, it is seldom to your advantage to begin by placing Kudzu on an opposing land.

Instead, place it on one of your lands which has been afflicted with a deleterious Enchantment. When you next tap that land, it is destroyed, and you can move Kudzu on to an opposing land. The obvious targets should be specialty lands, or those which an opponent can ill afford to see destroyed.

When using Kudzu, it's best to make extensive use of non-land sources of mana, limiting the impact when Kudzu comes back to haunt you. Indeed, this is another method of using Kudzu. When you have acquired enough Llanowar Elves, Birds of Paradise and Fyndhorn Elders to support your mana needs, cast Kudzu and forget about the consequences. As your opponent slowly, inexorably loses his or her land, you can rely on other sources of mana. This particular tactic works best when combined with the effects of Armageddon. With your non-land sources of mana, cast Kudzu on the first land you bring into play. Your opponent will then put a land into play. On your next turn, tap your land when casting a spell and place Kudzu on the opposing land. This in effect limits your opponent to using one land for the rest of the duel.

If your opponent is not cooperating and refuses to tap the land which is enchanted by Kudzu, you can always use the Icy Manipulator, Twiddle or the Elder Druid to force him or her to do so, setting off the spell.

Kudzu is, obviously, best used in a particular set of circumstances and will not benefit every spellbook in which it is placed. Care and prudence must be exercised before this enchantment can be of use to you.

The Lord of the Mountain looked at the clouds which were funneling in the sky above and muttered darkly to himself. The ghostly red aura which always seemed to surround him flared briefly, and the vines entrapping his feet disintegrated.

"The lengths to which Canticle will go to perpetuate a hoax never cease to amaze me."

Stalking over to his dazed assistant, the Lord of the Mountain picked him up by his collar.

"That spider and those vines constitute a game misconduct."

Dutifully, the goblin picked up his quill and writing parchment and jotted down the infractions.

Living Artifact

(Alpha, Beta, Unlimited, Revised, 4th Edition)

Card Name: **Living Artifact**
Color: **Green**
Spell Type: **Enchant Artifact**
Casting Cost: **G**
P/T: -

Put 1 counter on target artifact per life you lose. During upkeep, you may trade one and only one counter for 1 life.

Below decks on the Royal Barque, the Queen of Cameshbaan reclined on a pile of black silk cushions, attended to by the scaly green monstrosity which she called her companion. The storm beyond the confines of her quarters was of little concern to her, spells and enchantments keeping her in comfort as slaves and servants toiled to keep the vessel afloat.

"Such a surprise I'll have for them all, won't I, my pet?"

The ogre grunted, nodding as it refilled her wine glass. Smiling elegantly, flipping a stray braid from in front of her face, she gestured to a darkened corner with her cup. Drops of wine splashed on the floor as she spoke.

*"They certainly won't be expecting that. Hassan never did think such things were my style." A look of pure disgust crossed her face as a tentacle writhed. Hung from the ceiling in the corner, ensconced in a steel cage, was the squirming, undulating mass of a **Living Artifact**.*

Costing 1 Green mana, this spell may be used to enchant any single artifact in play. The Artifact acquires a vitality counter for each point of damage which is dealt to you. During your upkeep, a vitality counter may be removed, and you gain 1 life. Unfortunately, this ability may only be used once during each upkeep.

One of the more important decisions to make when casting Living Artifact is where to place it. Since the Enchantment is only useful so long as it survives, it should never be put in a position where it may be easily destroyed. As a result, artifacts like the Ivory Tower, Black Vise and the Winter Orb are usually the best choices. Especially if those

Artifacts belong to your opponent. Targeting an opponent's artifacts means that in order to get rid of the Living Artifact, chances are he or she will have to destroy his or her own artifact to do it.

Once in play, there exists the problem of how to maximize the use of Living Artifact. A favorite tactic is to employ creatures which deal damage to both players, and place a Spirit Link on them. If a Spirit Link is placed on the Brothers of Fire, Orcish Artillery or even the Cuombajj Witches, a large number of vitality counters can be generated without a net loss of life. All of these creatures are still dealing damage to you—it's simply being cancelled by means of Spirit Link. Slightly more complex, but just as useful, is the use of Spirit Link on an opposing creature, then using the Nettling Imp or Norrit to force it into an attack.

Keep in mind that the Living Artifact can at best provide you with only 1 life point a turn. In and of itself, this may not seem like much, but combined with the effects of an Ivory Tower, or a Stream of Life, it can be the decisive edge in a duel. The presence of a Living Artifact allows you to negate the effects of small, nettlesome attacks, which can be allowed through to generate vitality. If an opponent attacks with a large number of creatures, allowing a 1/1 through to make better use of blockers becomes a viable option.

While the edge that Living Artifact provides is a small one, it is the small advantages which can prove most important in the end. With multiple Living Artifacts in play, you can even begin accumulating life rather than simply avoiding damage.

"Do cover that thing up, it's beginning to drip. . . ."

The ogre moved towards the cage obediently, a black velvet sheet draped over its arm. With a flourish, it covered the Living Artifact's cage, shielding it from the delicate and sensitive eyes of his mistress. The Queen sipped at her wine, tilting her head as if to listen to a distant sound.

"Why, I do believe that we're almost there. Do have the captain toss one of the slaves overboard, as thanks for our safe arrival."

Ley Druid

(Alpha, Beta, Unlimited, Revised, 4th Edition)

In the woods south of the Mourning Lands, there stands what was once a monument to life itself. A ring of stones, covered with moss and pitted with the ravages of time, stands within an overgrown clearing. Within the ring, a stone table sits, crawling with ivy. Perpetual twilight, courtesy of the Beast, reigns over Torwynn, bathing the clearing in an unnatural light. Despite the horrors crossing the length and breadth of the world, however, this single spot seems tranquil and at peace.

Circling the stones, deep in contemplation, the solitary keeper of the grove walks, last of the ***Ley Druids****.*

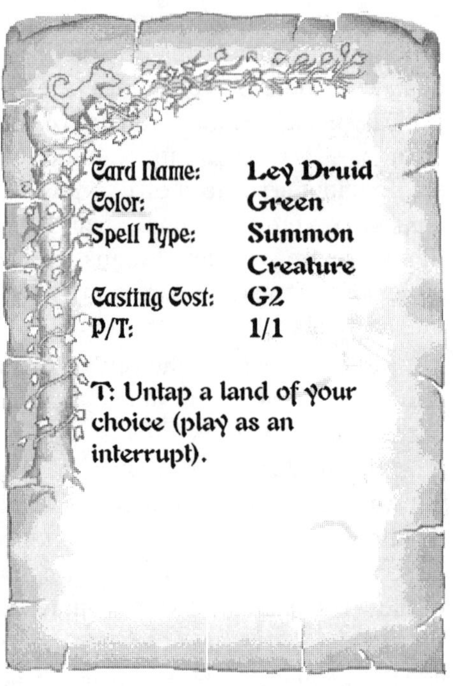

As creatures of the wood go, the Druid is somewhat expensive, a 1/1 costing 1 Green mana and 2 Colorless. When tapped, the Ley Druid can untap a land of your choice.

The most immediate benefits imparted by the Ley Druid are obvious. Since the Druid's ability to untap a land is considered an interrupt, the Ley Druid can be used to provide additional mana for spells. For example, if you have 2 Forests in play, one with a Wild Growth, the Ley Druid allows you to access 5 mana. After you have tapped the lands for mana, untap the Wild Growth-ed Forest using the Druid, and then tap it again. Equally frightening for your opponent is the prospect of untapping Urza's Lands while one of each is in play. Urza's Tower, for example, can be tapped for 3 mana, untapped using the Ley Druid, and then tapped for 3 more, yielding 6 mana from one land for one spell.

The Ley Druid also allows you to access the powers of special lands more than once a turn. The Maze of Ith, for example, can be untapped as an Interrupt, and then used again to untap another attacking creature. The Library of Alexandria can be used twice in one turn, while lands which have beneficial enchantments such as Earthlore on them can be accessed multiple times to provide that much more benefit.

In a Stasis Deck, a Ley Druid with Instill Energy can allow you to access mana while your opponent remains crippled. In a variation on the Stasis theme, the Ley Druid provides an excellent method of pulling out from under the effects of a Winter Orb. Rather than untapping only one land a turn, the Ley Druid allows you to untap two or three, depending on whether it has Instill Energy, or whether you're making use of multiple Druids. Adding another twist to this tactic is the use of the Ley Druid in a Power Surge strategy. Use the Druid to untap your opponent's lands before the end of your turn, forcing your opponent to take additional damage. When using detrimental enchantments such as Psychic Venom, the Ley Druid can also be used to excellent effect. For example, if you have a Mana Short in hand, untap a Psychic Venomed land before casting it.

The Ley Druid is a fragile creature, however, and its considerable uses make it a very appealing target. Wards are well worth considering on the Ley Druid, for it is truly an investment worth protecting.

The Druid stopped in his tracks, turning his gaze to the starless sky. Throwing back his hood, he shook loose his long black locks and sighed. In the shadows of the wood, his features seemed delicate, almost elfin, his eyes glinting strangely. A pendant, a unicorn's head, perhaps, glittered briefly as he turned towards the stone table in the center of the ring.

"Master, I shall do what I can to aid you."

Lifeforce
(Alpha, Beta, Unlimited, Revised, 4th Edition)

Kneeling before the table, the druid removed a small handful of herbs from a satchel, scattering them over the ivy wrapped stone surface. Musical phrases danced over his lips as he recited a liturgy of praise to the wood and its long vanished protector.

In the air above the table, a pulsing orb of pale green light began to grow in intensity, drawing upon the energies of the wood itself, drawing power from its ***Lifeforce****.*

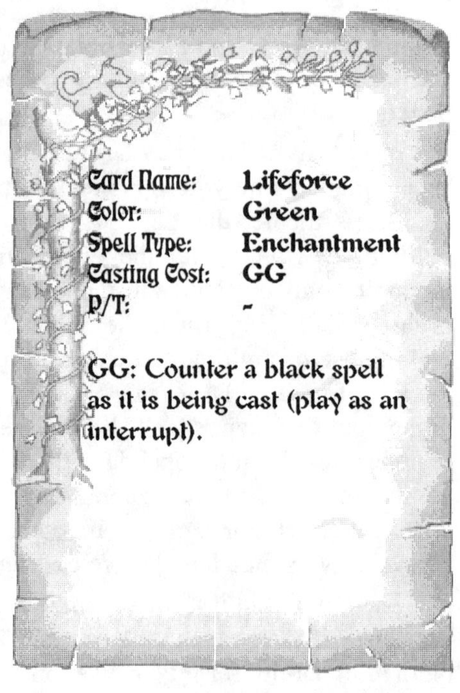

At a cost of 2 Green mana, this Enchantment can prove to be one of the most valuable available to a Green Mage. When 2 Green mana are spent, a target black spell may be countered as it is being cast. Played at the speed of an interrupt, this ability provides Green with powers it previously could not hope to access.

The power of this Enchantment cannot be understated, as it gives Green the ability to counter spells. Simply setting aside a Wild Growthed Forest will allow you to counter any one Black spell as it is being cast. With more forests available, the ability to do damage to a Black Mage increases. Indeed, once Lifeforce is in play, a mage who relies on spells of Black is crippled, as the magicks of Green generally allow access to larger pools of mana. Combining the effects of Wild Growth and a Ley Druid, for example, can allow you to use one land to effectively counter up to 2 Black spells in a single turn.

Lifeforce can be even more useful when combined with Sleight of Mind. In this case, it can be used to counter spells of the color of your choice. With two Lifeforces in play, one Sleighted to an alternate color, almost any practitioner of Black magicks can be completely shut down. Lifeforce is an Enchantment, and is incapable of being countered by the traditional methods of Power Sink, Counterspell or Spell Blast once it is in play. Sleight can also be used as a surprise tactic, as it is legal for you to wait until your opponent is casting a spell, discern which color he or she is using, then interrupt by sleighting Lifeforce to the appropriate color.

Getting rid of Lifeforce once it enters play is a difficult proposition, at best. Any Black spells which could have an impact on Lifeforce will, no doubt, face immediate countering, which makes use of a backup color all the more important. Blue allows you to use Power Leak, White has Disenchant, while Green itself has Tranquility. A Sleighted Lifeforce, however, can deal with these threats as well.

The Orb throbbed, flashing brilliantly as it sensed the Beast drawing mana forth from the forest. Far in the distance, beneath Easthold, the Beast let loose a bellow of rage as it discovered the powers of the wood denied to it.

The Druid smiled thinly, turning his back on the Orb and the table, returning to his self imposed exile in the wood. For a time, at least, these lands would once again be safe from the ancient evil. Now it was up to his master.

"Farewell, Canticle."

Lure

(Alpha, Beta, Unlimited, Revised, 4th Edition, Ice Age)

"Spirits above and below. . . . "

Siward looked over the prow of the boat at the scene which was laid out before him. A swampy morass was all that was left of the village, save for a few scattered timbers and the bloated bodies of the dead. Bandares simply shrugged his shoulders, and ordered the crew to begin unloading the vessel.

"Wait! There's someone over there . . . . "

Bandares turned to follow Siward's pointing finger. Already, several members of the crew were slogging through what was left of the village, towards the lone figure on the hilltop. His features fell, and he began cursing magnificently.

"You FOOLS! It's a trap! A ***Lure****!"*

Card Name:	**Lure**
Color:	**Green**
Spell Type:	**Enchant Creature**
Casting Cost:	**GG1**
P/T:	**-**

All creatures that can block target creature must do so.

A creature enchantment costing 2 Green mana and 1 Colorless, the Lure is a potent weapon indeed. Once in effect, all creatures which the Lure-bearing beast faces on the attack are required to block, drawn by its irresistible pull.

One of the most common and effective combinations with the Lure is with the Thicket Basilisk, something which is often referred to as the creature sweeper. When thrown into battle, a Lured Basilisk will destroy absolutely every creature other than a wall in its path. There are even methods of avoiding the destruction of the Basilisk in the process. Darkness, Fog or similar magics will prevent all damage as a result of combat from taking effect, but will not prevent the destruction of creatures which blocked the Basilisk.

Black Mages have a similar combination available to them in the Infernal Medusa. The Abomination is useful to a lesser extent, as the colors which it impacts are more restricted, but should be considered nonetheless. Black, however, possesses an even more devastating combination involving Lure—The Wretched. Imagine a situation where a Lured Wretched attacks, and you then cast Darkness to prevent damage from taking place. Every defending creature comes under your control, a situation sure to give your foe pause.

One can even jury-rig the Thicket Basilisk/Lure combination through the use of the Venom enchantment on a creature. In this manner, one can mimic the ability of the Basilisk without actually having to bring one into play.

The Lure is not limited to use as a creator of creature sweeping combinations, however. Any color can make effective use of the Lure, depending on the situation. For example, placing Lure on a Regenerating creature before an attack can cause a great deal of consternation on the part of an opponent. Lure on the Drudge Skeletons can be devastating when those Skeletons are attacking in conjunction with the Murk Dwellers, for example. Use Lure on a paltry 1/1 creature and then throw it into the attack. After blockers have been declared, use the Maze of Ith to untap that creature, keeping it safe for use again and again.

Another method one can use to foul the defense of an opponent is through the use of the Aisling Leprechaun and Lure. Place a Lure on the Leprechaun, and the use a Lace to change the color of the Lure to something other than Green. At this point, apply a Green Ward. Once this has been completed, you have a 1/1 creature which turns all defenders into Green creatures, which are incapable of harming the Leprechaun. If you have a Circle of Protection: Green in play, you can secure a victory in this manner.

Finding a way to deal with Lure is somewhat more difficult, especially if you do not possess anti-enchantment magicks. Anything blocking a Lured creature usually does so at some great cost. More creative methods of avoiding the effects of Lured beasts are usually needed than simply blocking the beast. Using the Dwarven Warriors to render the Lured creature unblockable, casting Flight on it so it cannot be blocked by land-bound creatures, or even casting Invisibility or Fear on it may be preferable to allowing the creature to make use of its abilities.

Siward spun around to face Bandares, surprise and fear on his face. A trap? He turned his attention back towards the hill. By now, the entire crew was making its way through the remains of the village, fighting their way to the figure which stood alone on the hilltop. His jaw nearly dropped from his skull as he watched each member of the crew slowly stop moving, held immobile by some eldritch power. And then they began to sink into the muddy grounds of the village.

Within moments, they had disappeared to a man. The figure on the hilltop was silhouetted briefly against the sky, and then disappeared.

Metamorphosis

(Arabian Nights, Chronicles)

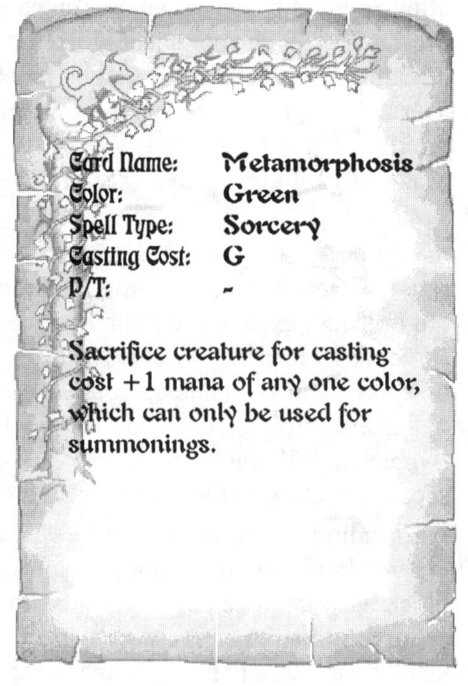

Bandares smacked his hand against the rail and stalked down the gangplank onto the dock. The rotting wooden frame bobbed beneath his weight, but he paid little attention to it, instead directing his diminutive, impish assistant to take hold of the large bronze casket which had been left unattended on the beach.

"Siward. . . ."

The young apprentice came down and stood next to Bandares. The older man put his arm around Siward's shoulder and began walking towards the remains of the village.

"Well, we've finally made it. Now, for some fun. . . ."

Siward fell to his knees on the beach, hands flying to his throat as he gasped for breath. His eyes felt like they were about to burst from their sockets, and he realized that he was undergoing some sort of ***Metamorphosis****.*

A 1 Green mana sorcery, this spell allows you to sacrifice one of your creatures in play and receive an amount of mana equal to that creature's casting cost, plus 1. This mana may only be of one color, however, and may only be used to summon creatures.

In order to get the most mileage out of this spell, it is highly recommended that you use your opponent's creatures as fodder. Using methods such as Old Man of the Sea, Preacher, Aladdin for artifact creatures or Seasinger can allow you to take control of an opponent's forces. You can then use Metamorphosis to bring out creatures from your hand without tapping out your lands. Not only will you be denying use of a creature to your opponent, but you will also be able to bring a creature complete under your control into play, without having to worry about it returning to your foe.

Another favored method of using Metamorphosis is in conjunction with Enduring Renewal. Since the sacrificed creature simple returns to your hand, you have a wide variety of options available to you. For example, if you have an Abomination and Enduring Renewal in play, 2 Plains, and 3 Swamps, with a Fallen Angel and an Infernal Medusa in hand, you would normally be able to bring out only one of those creatures. Not so with Metamorphosis. Use it on the Abomination, and you can cast the Fallen Angel. Tap your lands to summon the Medusa, and the Abomination returns to your hand for use next turn. This principle holds true in a wide variety of situations, giving you two creatures for the price of one.

Using Metamorphosis on creatures which benefit you in death is another popular tactic. Casting Metamorphosis on a Rukh Egg, for example, provides you with a 4/4 flying creature and 5 mana with which to summon another creature. Blazing Effigy, Onulet, and even Su-Chi can all be destroyed with Metamorphosis for the same reasons.

Metamorphosis is also useful in bringing out creatures when you simply don't have the proper mana available otherwise. Consider a situation, not uncommon, where you have 4 Forests in play and a handful of Red creatures. Sacrifice your Grizzly Bears with Metamorphosis, and you can have access to Red mana for the purposes of summoning.

Siward fell to the ground, twitching and convulsing, hands digging into the sand. Tears scrabbled down his cheeks as he looked up at his erstwhile master, and he managed to choke out a single word before dying.

"Why?"

Bandares looked down at the corpse of the young sailor, a youth who in another time and place may have served him well.

"Because I can."

Naf's Asp

(Arabian Nights, 4th Edition)

Card Name:	Naf's Asp
Color:	Green
Spell Type:	Summon Creature
Casting Cost:	G
P/T:	1/1

If Naf's Asp hits opponent, it does 1 point of damage during opponent's next upkeep unless 1 is paid.

The Royal Barque Of Martuk, bearing with it her Imperial Tarkheena, the Sorceress Queen of Cameshbaan, reached port in Easthold with all the dignity of a leper.

Sails hung limply from broken masts, while timbers warped away from the hull in alarming fashion. Two thirds of the crew had been washed overboard, while the captain, unable to explain the sudden loss of manpower to her majesty, had been sacrificed to the sea spirits in place of a slave.

The Queen ignored it all, treading delicately down the gangplank to meet with a man who referred to himself as the Burgh of the village of Ghant. She snorted in derision as she repeated the names to herself. Such appropriately flatulent names for such a backwater place.

The Burgh, a portly man in his fifties, bowed elaborately as the Queen and her Ogre escort stepped onto the dock. His eyes bulged alarmingly, and he let loose a short yelp of pain. Looking down, he saw a large snake slithering back towards the Queen.

"First, and most important, your bow was inadequate. Second, your title offends my sensibilities." Bending down, she picked up ***Naf's Asp****.*

At a cost of 1 Green mana, this 1/1 creature is insidiously powerful. If damage is inflicted upon your opponent by this creature, he or she must pay 1 mana before the draw phase of his or her next turn, or lose an additional 1 point of life. Note that this damage will continue to take place until the 1 mana cost is paid.

At such a low cost, Naf's Asp is certainly among the most effective 1/1 creatures which you can utilize in the duel. Among the practitioners of Black Magicks, a strategy has developed which has proven to be incredibly useful. Using the powers of The Fallen, Murk Dwellers, and Naf's Asp, a deadly combination has been created. All of these beasts are capable of dealing additional damage to your opponent should they remain unblocked, and the combination of all three can quickly prove devastating. Add Hypnotic Specters to the mix, and you create an army which requires blocking at all costs.

In such a situation, it is imperative that the Asp reach its target unblocked, and a wide variety of magicks can be used to facilitate this. Using Dwarven Warriors or Tawnos's Wand is the most immediately obvious way, though Invisibility and Fear can serve almost as well. The combination of the Warriors and the Asp is one of the simplest, and most effective, since it forces your opponent to take 1 damage on the attack, and then choose to take another during his or her draw phase, or pay a mana to prevent it. With a Winter Orb in play, this choice becomes even less appealing than usual. Combined with Venom, Asp can become even more troublesome. If it is blocked, the blocking creature will die. If it is allowed through, the problem exists of whether to spend more mana or take more damage.

Granted, the Asp faces all the usual difficulties associated with 1/1 creatures. Easily slain, easily blocked, and more often than not, easily countered, the key to effective use of the Asp lies in striking hard, striking fast and most importantly, striking early.

The Queen looked down at the writhing Burgh, and spat on the planks next to his convulsing form.

"And finally, you nearly stepped on poor Nasid." Cooing to the snake, she stroked the back of its head as it hissed at the corpse. Tugging on the leash which kept her Ogre in check, she made her way into the village.

"Now let's find ourselves a Beast."

Regeneration

(Alpha, Beta, Unlimited, Revised, 4th Edition, Ice Age)

Picking through the undergrowth and brambles, the Lord of the Mountain muttered darkly to himself. Officials in sporting events simply weren't supposed to be subjected to this sort of thing. His unfortunate scribe hobbled along behind him, trying gamely to keep up with the infuriated mage.

Card Name: Regeneration
Color: Green
Spell Type: Enchant Creature
Casting Cost: G1
P/T: -

G: Target creature regenerates.

A loud explosion tossed the goblin back several yards as the Lord of the Mountain disappeared in a shower of sparks and lights. The bolt had descended from above, appearing out of a dreary, but otherwise calm, sky. The Lord of the Mountain stood there for a moment, staring at the stump which had been his left arm.

"Oh really, this has gone far enough."

The Lord of the Mountain sat there, tapping his foot impatiently while tendons, muscles and bone slowly grew back into place, a display of ***Regeneration****.*

Costing 1 Green mana and 1 Colorless, this Enchantment allows a creature to Regenerate with the activation cost of 1 Green mana.

Normally a province of Black Magicks, Regeneration provides a Mage with a wide variety of options when it comes to utilizing his or her creatures in the most efficient manner possible. As the Drudge Skeletons are so often used as renewable blockers, now a Green Mage can be privy to the same sort of annoying power. On the attack, a Regenerating Naf's Asp can tie up blockers. Your opponent won't want to allow it through, due to the nature of its ability, yet blocking it is almost pointless, since it will simply Regenerate.

Normally, Regeneration is placed on those creatures which are so valuable to your efforts that you wish to expend as much energy as possible in protecting them. Ley Druids, Sorceress Queens, Prodigal Sorcerers and Trackers all fall into this sort of category. With Regeneration and the spare mana to power it, you no longer have to worry about spells like Lightning Bolt, Fireball, or artifacts such as the Rod of Ruin destroying carefully laid plans in an instant. There are more subtle ways in which to put Regeneration to use, however.

By placing it on a creature such as the Thicket Basilisk, or on one which has been enchanted with Venom, you create a killing machine that just keeps coming back. When you enchant The Wretched, you have a situation where every turn, the defenders end up on your side, and damage dealt to The Wretched becomes irrelevant. With Giant Albatross, you can force an opponent to lose his or her creatures, or expend mana. Add a Winter Orb to this particular combination to make the choice even harder for your opponent. By the same token, using Regeneration on creatures like the Shimian Night Stalker, Veteran Bodyguard, or Martyrs of Korlis extends their usefulness. If they die taking damage on your behalf, simply Regenerate them and they can be reused in the same manner. Placing Regeneration on the Tracker can be useful as well. The Karplusan Yeti can be enchanted in the same way.

In rare cases, it may even be beneficial to place Regeneration on opposing creatures. Since the Enchantment remains under your control, you choose when to activate it. For example, if an opposing creature has Wanderlust on it, your foe may do all in his or her power to destroy it. Place Regeneration on that creature, and you create a situation where your opponent is trying to destroy his own creature while you are trying to protect it. Putting it on a Juzam Djinn or a Serendib Efreet after it has been rendered harmless by means of a Circle of Protection or Gaseous Form is another example.

After a few moments, the Lord of the Mountain was once again complete. He tugged at the scorched edges of his robes, seared off at the shoulder, and sighed. Pushing aside brush and twigs, he made off once again down the wooded slope, dictating to his scribe.

"Note. The Beast may exist after all."

Sandstorm

(Arabian Nights, 4th Edition)

The small boat carrying Canticle, El-Hajjaj, Ariana and an unknown number of gremlins touched ground on the northern coast of Easthold, beaching itself on the sandy shores north of Pasch. The surrounding fields of heather were motionless in the dead air, not even the whisper of a breeze present. Looking south, the Necromancer shook his head. Torrential rains were pounding the landscape not more than an hour's march away.

Card Name: Sandstorm
Color: Green
Spell Type: Instant
Casting Cost: G
P/T: -

Do 1 damage to all attacking creatures.

"Ariana!"

Canticle turned at El-Hajjaj's shout in time to witness a black clad figure emerging from below decks, directly behind the exhausted Ariana. Before either he or El-Hajjaj could move, a blade was at her throat.

"This time. Black One, there shall be a reckoning."

As Canticle's gremlins leapt towards Hassan, the very beach seemed to rise up and descend upon the boat. The gremlins were buried in the ***Sandstorm****.*

At a cost of 1 Green mana, this Instant deals 1 damage to all attacking creatures. Simple, brutal, and effective, it has proven its worth time and again in battle.

When used against the infamous "Weenie Horde" strategy, Sandstorm can be devastating. An army of Savannah Lions, Benalish Heroes, and Mesa Pegasi can be wiped out with a single spell. Add D'Avenant Archers, Crimson Manticores, Deserts, and the Maze of Ith to the mix, and attacking becomes a losing proposition. Combined with the above lands and creatures, Sandstorm can be used to take out any attacking creatures with a toughness of up to 3. The surprise aspect of Sandstorm is also effective in this respect; when calculating for an attack, an opponent may take an Archer or Desert into consideration, but unless he or she knows what's in your hand, Sandstorm can be a deciding factor.

Since Sandstorm is only effective against attacking creatures, however, there may be situations where you will want to entice your opponent into attacking. While Nettling Imps and Norrits could be used to entice creatures over piecemeal, the use of Sandstorm in such efforts is almost a waste of time. However, with multiple Sandstorms, or when combined with creatures such as those mentioned previously, other spells become much more useful. Siren's Call and Season of the Witch, for example, can be used to force an opponent to attack under less than ideal conditions. Casting a Sandstorm or two after Siren's Call can humble an opponent, putting him or her at a severe disadvantage when it comes to armies.

In a Green/White spellbook, there is even an application for Sandstorm against your own forces, as odd as it may seem. The tactic also has use when Sandstorm is used against you, so it bears mentioning. After casting Blood of the Martyr, damage to your creatures may be redirected to you instead. After Sandstorm has resolved, cast Reverse Damage.

A gremlin clambered to its feet in front of Ariana, spitting sand onto the deck, shaking its fuzzy form to remove the irritant from its flesh. Hassan looked down with bemusement, slowly moving his blade away from Ariana's throat as he addressed the Necromancer.

"It is an old debt, Black One, and it must be paid. . . ."

The Ashashid gestured to the immense funnel in the skies above Easthold with his scimitar.

"But there are older, more expensive debts at hand."

Scryb Sprites
(Alpha, Beta, Unlimited, Revised, 4th Edition)

The Lord of the Mountain and his ever faithful servant reached the valley floor relatively intact, although the Mage complained bitterly about the state of his robes. The goblin continued taking notations, swatting idly at oversized insects which buzzed about his head.

Card Name:	Scryb Sprites
Color:	Green
Spell Type:	Summon Creature
Casting Cost:	G
P/T:	1/1

Flying.

It wasn't long before the Lord of the Mountain realized that something about the wooded valley wasn't quite right. The air carried the scent of pine and larch, and was filled with the sound of birds and chittering squirrels. Snapping his fingers, he practically shouted out his realization.

"Nothing's dead! OW!"

Swatting at his cheek, the Lord of the Mountain pulled a small dart from his flesh. The winged insects had grown more aggressive, apparently. And more intelligent, for they seemed to be wearing clothes. In seconds, the Lord of the Mountain and his scribe were under attack by ***Scryb Sprites****.*

1 Green mana is all that's required to bring these 1/1 flying creatures into play, a quality which has endeared them to many woodland Magi. Long looked down upon for their delicate, almost simplistic nature, these creatures can prove to be the focal point of a duel when properly utilized.

As flying creatures go, the Scryb Sprites are among the cheapest ones available, discounting the defensively oriented Ornithopter. This aspect makes them a key part of the "Green Horde" method of duelling, a tactic which relies on fast mana and cheap creatures. A second turn Mountain after a first turn Forest provides you with some excellent options involving the Scryb Sprites, realistic and viable. Cast Blood Lust on the Sprites, followed by Giant Growth, and you have a temporary 8/4 flying creature on the second turn. A Giant Growth or Blood Lust alone is adequate to put you ahead in the duel.

With a simple Regeneration, Scryb Sprites provide Green with something it is sorely lacking—adequate air cover. Serra Angels and Fallen Angels may be frightening, but with a Regenerating flyer blocking their path, you can buy yourself time until a more permanent method of dealing with them can be arranged. Tag a Venom on the Sprites as well, and you have an offensive powerhouse for a low price.

Scryb Sprites also benefit due to their very nature as cheap, low-power flyers. While they are effective on the attack in the early stages of the duel, they are often overlooked as more powerful creatures enter the battle. Few Magi want to waste a Terror or a Fissure on Scryb Sprites when they are being threatened by Scaled Wurms. It is this inherent frailty that often proves their greatest asset. Using the Dwarven Warriors to make them unblockable, Scryb Sprites and a Howl From Beyond can end things in rapid fashion. The fast nature of Green magick makes this all the more likely as well. With an abundance of Wild Growths, Llanowar Elves and Ley Druids, a fourth or fifth turn Sprite with Howl From Beyond could be dealing 10 damage. Add to this mixture the powers of the Faerie Noble, and you have a creature with the potential to become incredibly dangerous.

Despite its frail nature, never underestimate the power of Scryb Sprites. Sometimes the most effective weapon is the one which appears most harmless.

Swatting and waving his arms, the Lord of the Mountain attempted to fend off the sprites while weaving a spell at the same time. While his original intention had been to erect a wall of fire to keep them away, he ended up encapsulating both himself and his scribe in a hollow, transparent sphere. The Sprites beat angrily on the surface of the sphere, their tiny fists having little impact on a construct of magick. The goblin scribe stuck his tongue out at one sprite, putting thumb to his nose and waggling his fingers.

The Lord of the Mountain sat there with his chin in hands, elbows in lap. He hadn't the first idea how to dispel the sphere.

Titania's Song
(Antiquities, Revised, 4th Edition)

Night fell in the strangely vibrant valley, bringing with it the sounds and sights associated with it. Apart from the hovering sphere containing the Lord of the Mountain and his dozing assistant, everything seemed tranquil.

The Lord of the Mountain cocked his head as if straining to catch a distant sound. Over the chirping of insects and the padding of paw over brush, he heard something else, something new. A lilting voice carrying on an ancient wind. Although the voice was unfamiliar, he recognized the chant, and finally the words. Here, in the midst of the island which had birthed the Beast, someone was singing ***Titania's Song****.*

Card Name:	**Titania's Song**
Color:	**Green**
Spell Type:	**Enchantment**
Casting Cost:	**G3**
P/T:	-

Every non-creature artifact in play loses its usual abilities and becomes an artifact creature with power and toughness equal to its casting cost. Should Titania's Song leave play, artifacts revert to normal just before the next turn's untap phase.

An Enchantment of incredible power, 1 Green mana and 3 Colorless are all that is needed to bring it into play. While active, Titania's Song turns all non-creature Artifacts into artifact creatures with a power and toughness equivalent to their casting cost. At the same time, they lose all of their usual abilities.

Titania's Song is most often used by those who despise and abhor the Artificers, a method by which their mechanized toys may be fouled and rendered useless. Favored victims of this spell are the Moxen, Loti and other 0 casting cost artifacts—so long as Titania's Song is in play, casting these artifacts simply guarantees their destruction. In this respect, getting the Song out early is the most effective method of using it. With a wide variety of fast mana available, it can usually enter play by at least the third turn.

Titania's Song is not just useful as a method to prevent low-cost artifacts from entering play. It can prove deadly to those artifacts which have a casting cost as well. The Throne of Bone, Wooden Sphere and similar artifacts, along with the Ivory Tower and Black Vise will all lose their abilities and find themselves highly vulnerable to the effects of the Prodigal Sorcerer or Tracker as a result of Titania's Song. The favored combination of the Ivory Tower and Library of Leng is stopped in its tracks by Titania's Song, as is the Black Vise/Rack pairing.

There are ways to utilize Titania's Song offensively as well. High-cost artifacts which are no longer useful to your cause may be rendered inert and turned into attackers and defenders by means of Titania's Song. The Armageddon Clock, Aladdin's Lamp, the Book of Rass and Standing Stones can all be used as effective, high-power and toughness creatures once their usual abilities become more of a liability than a benefit. Care should also be exercised in the later stages of a duel against an Artificer: while his 6 casting cost Armageddon Clock may not be used as originally intended, a 6/6 creature is not a paltry thing to have to deal with.

The song grew louder and seemed to surround the sphere which contained the Lord of the Mountain and his scribe from all sides. Grasping his robes, the Lord looked over to the goblin with a resigned sigh. . . .

POP

The sphere disappeared, dropping its contents unceremoniously into the nettles and bushes below. Attempting to maintain an air of dignity, the Lord of the Mountain began picking thorns from his clothing, while the scribe simply whimpered.

"You realize, of course, that there are some days when it simply doesn't pay to get up in the morning."

Tsunami

(Alpha, Beta, Unlimited, Revised, 4th Edition)

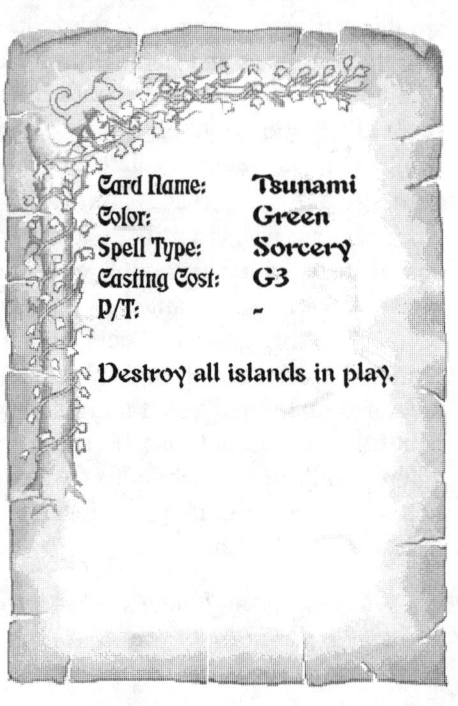

Bandares sat at the top of the hillock, looking out over the ocean, whistling a tuneless little ditty to himself over and over again. An ivory-handled knife was in his hand, and he was using it to carve intricate swirls and shapes into a piece of driftwood. His withered assistant was dragging a large bronze box to the top of the hill, stopping every so often to adjust his lumpen hat. Bandares nodded as he reached the summit.

"Finished?"

Tugging at his wispy beard, his assistant dipped his head in acknowledgment. Bandares smiled, getting to his feet.

"Let's play God."

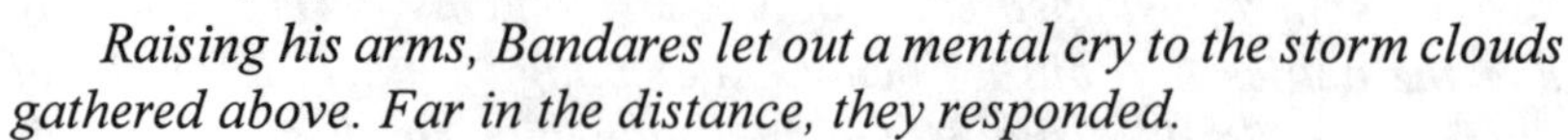

Raising his arms, Bandares let out a mental cry to the storm clouds gathered above. Far in the distance, they responded.

The sound was like rolling thunder, only it continued to grow in strength and intensity. In the distance, a wall of water rose up against the horizon, washing towards shore, an inexorable ***Tsunami****.*

At a cost of 1 Green mana and 3 Colorless, this Sorcery destroys all Islands in play. A devastating spell, it is deceivingly simple in appearance.

While Tsunami can be an effective method of crippling a Blue Mage, the problem exists of getting this spell to properly fire. No sane and rational practitioner of Blue will allow the successful casting of Tsunami, often going so far as forever keeping 2 Islands untapped for a Counterspell when facing Green. And the fear is justified. A Tsunami cast on the third or fourth turn can set the stage for victory, as the loss of resources is often too much to overcome. Effective use of Tsunami demands that the casting mage prevent the casting of counterspells at all costs. A favored method is using the Elder Druid to tap Islands which may be used to power a counterspell, and using the Icy Manipulator to do the same. If Red is being used in conjunction with Green, hold back a few Red Elemental Blasts just in case.

Another effective method of getting Tsunami into play is using it after having put Monsoon out. Monsoon provides an opponent with the incentive to tap his or her islands, and when this is done, Tsunami can be used to destroy them. Alternately, Monsoon can be used as the decoy, and when it is counterspelled or spell blasted, Tsunami can take effect.

Tsunami also has applications in a Blue/Green spellbook, as contradictory as it may seem. With Magical Hack, the text on Tsunami can be altered to a land type used by your opponent. In this manner, Tsunami can become a method of land destruction that your opponent may never see coming. What Mountain Mage expects his resources to be flooded by a Tsunami?

The Tsunami crashed down on the shores of Easthold with the force of a thousand winds, smashing timbers into kindling, throwing boulders and bricks in all directions, showering the lands for a league in all directions with mud.

Bandares and his assistant watched the entire scene from the safety of a force field, erected moments before the Tsunami hit. Running his hands through his hair, he turned to face the interior of the island. Raising his hand to the sky, gesturing obscenely, he began to laugh.

"Call yourself the Beast? You're just an amateur."

Red Spells

Ali Baba

(Arabian Nights, 4th Edition)

Reclining against a veritable wall of cushions, the Queen of Cameshbaan did her best to relax in her new surroundings. Her minions had been at work in the mountains all day, with little to show for their efforts, and her mood was beginning to sour. She was hoping that she wouldn't have to rely on the services of an itinerant thief but had brought him on the voyage just in case. Now it appeared he would be needed, and he was late.

An oversized green vest was worn over his faded saffron robe, and he stroked his carelessly trimmed beard nervously as he entered. On the streets of Cameshbaan, his name was legendary among the lower classes, but now he was standing before the Queen, in a far-off land.

"I have need of you, ***Ali Baba****."*

Card Name:	**Ali Baba**
Color:	**Red**
Spell Type:	**Summon Creature**
Casting Cost:	**R**
P/T:	**1/1**

R: Tap a wall.

At a cost of 1 Red mana, this 1/1 individual can prove to be a valuable asset in your endeavors. When activated, Ali Baba may tap any number of target walls at a cost of 1 Red mana apiece.

While many consider this ability a pale reflection of that possessed by the Dwarven Demolition Team, nothing could be further from the truth. Ali Baba may use his ability numerous times in a turn, since tapping is not part of the activation cost. This kind of power can be invaluable before launching an assault. By spending three or four red mana, an equivalent number of walls can be taken out of action, leaving an opponent next to defenseless. Against those Magi who place too much emphasis on the defensive nature of Walls, Ali Baba can prove to be a crippling adversary. On the defensive, Ali Baba can prove valuable if your opponent makes use of enchantments like Animate Wall, or uses monstrosities like the Walking Wall. An added benefit of his power is the fact that he can launch an attack after using his power, or be put into use as a defender. While Enchantments of one sort or another would be required to insure his survival, it does expand his applications.

Against some of the more popular Walls, Ali Baba can prove to be even more crippling. Wall of Spears and the Living Wall are particularly susceptible to enchantment by Artifact Possession, at which point Ali Baba may be used to tap them and inflict 2 points of damage. If you have the Hyperion Blacksmith, you can untap the Wall, and then use Ali Baba to tap it yet again, for a total of 4 damage. While this tactic isn't exactly simple to institute, it can prove devastating. Multiple Artifact Possessions on a single wall not only deal damage as a result of Ali Baba's actions, but while tapped the walls are useless on defense. Add a Powerleech into the equation just for fun, as each tapping of the artifact will provide you with life.

In certain situations, Ali Baba can also be used to defend against the power of Glyphs. Consider a situation where someone decides to place a Glyph of Destruction on a blocking wall, sure that the result will be in his favor. Using Ali Baba, you can tap that wall, which will ultimately be destroyed due to the nature of the Glyph.

"You are my Queen, noble one, I shall do what is in my power. . . ."

The Queen smiled wickedly, and languidly waved her hand in the direction of the mountains.

"Somewhere up there, this deliciously wicked Beast is causing problems. My companion has found a cavern, but his. . .intellect. . .is not up to the task of discovering how to gain entry. You shall assist."

Ali Baba tried to hide the fact that he was shaking, hurriedly bowed, and turned to do the bidding of his Queen.

Atog
(Antiquities, Revised)

The cavern was damp and moist, more than likely a result of the torrential rains which had been falling almost perpetually on the southern side of Easthold. Water gathered in dank, stagnant pools on the floor, and the air was thick and cloying.

Card Name:	Atog
Color:	Red
Spell Type:	Summon Creature
Casting Cost:	R1
P/T:	1/2

0: +2/+2. Each time you use this ability, you must sacrifice one of your Artifacts in play.

Ali Baba made his way over rocks and boulders, trying not to think about the consequences of failure. The Queen was lavish in her rewards, and equally extravagant with her punishments.

*A high-pitched titter startled the thief, and he peered ahead into the darkness, holding his lantern up before him. A wide set of teeth broke into an inhuman grin, while a pair of bulbous eyes reflected the light. Ali Baba found himself staring directly at an **Atog**.*

A 1/2 creature costing 1 Red and 1 Colorless to summon, Atog possesses a unique power. Whenever an artifact is sacrificed to Atog, he gains +2/+2 until the end of the turn. This can be a potent ability.

Some of the more classic methods involved in making Atog an effective tool of battle involve the sacrifice of multiple artifacts. Use the Dwarven Warriors to make Atog unblockable. Then all available artifacts from the Ivory Tower to the Armageddon Clock can be sacrificed to him, pumping him up to appalling levels. The resulting damage is usually enough to end the duel then and there. Using 0 casting cost artifacts, this tactic can result in a large amount of damage in the very early stages of a duel. An Ornithopter and Urza's Bauble, sacrificed on the third turn to Atog, will give you access to a 5/6 attacker. With an Argivian Archaeologist in play, you can even recover those artifacts for later use. Another popular artifact for use with Atog is the Rocket Launcher. After use, it won't head to the graveyard until the end of the turn. Before that happens, just sacrifice it. If you're feeling nasty, use Enduring Renewal. The Ornithopter you just sacrificed returns to your hand, can be put into play, and sacrificed to Atog repeatedly ad infinitum. Endless power and toughness are not pleasant to face.

Perhaps one of the most frightening aspects of Atog, however, is the fact that he can be fed the creatures generated by The Hive and Serpent Generator—perpetual sources of power. Now there is no need to sacrifice a standard artifact to power Atog. For the price of a little mana, you can keep him healthy, happy, and ready to wreak havoc.

One of the most innovative and annoying uses for Atog involves feeding him your opponent's artifacts. Through the use of Aladdin, Scarwood Bandits, or in the case of Artifact Creatures, Old Man of the Sea and Preacher, you can acquire your opponent's valued artifacts for use as fodder. In this manner, you can bring a quick end to those artifacts which have become an irritant, and at the same time gain some added benefits.

Atog also benefits due to his toughness. While most specialty creatures suffer from an appallingly fragile constitution, Atog has a toughness of 2, putting him out of range of Prodigal Sorcerers, Rods of Ruin and other such nonsense. A simple Holy Armor will keep him safe from Lightning Bolts as well, while the addition of Ashnod's Transmogrant renders him immune from Terror, while increasing his power and toughness at the same time. In addition, the boost he receives from artifacts lasts the duration of the turn; perpetually feeding him keeps him at a level which should deter most destructive magics.

Rows of razor-sharp teeth glinted, and the purple hide of the creature glistened unwholesomely in the lantern's light. The same high-pitched titter echoed off the walls of the cavern, and Ali Baba dropped his satchel and light then and there. Before the last laugh had faded from his ears, he was scrambling down the side of the mountain.

Brothers of Fire
(The Dark, 4th Edition)

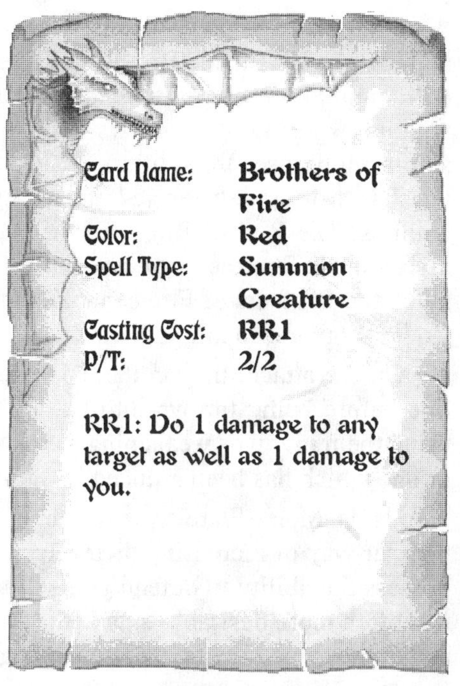

Bandares cursed, kicking aside a small boulder as he did so. The pillar that had been the object of his contest with Canticle, the objective of years of study, was nothing more than a pile of useless powder. The key to controlling the power of the Beast, one of the most subtle yet powerful artifacts ever devised, reduced to dust. A sudden realization dawned on Bandares as he examined the remnants of the pillar.

"This means that the Beast. . . ."

". . .be free to do wishes it wills, indeed."

Bandares spun around, arcane words on his lips. He faltered and blinked as he saw what stood before him. Apart from his assistant, he thought he had been alone on this desolate, boulder-strewn rock face. It was not the case, however. Before him stood a stunted, incredibly muscled man, with skin the color of liquid fire. Plated armour, constructed from solid granite, covered his vital organs, and he rested his weight on a spear which appeared to be crafted from obsidian. There wasn't a doubt in Bandares' mind that this was one of the ***Brothers of Fire****.*

At a cost of 2 Red mana and 1 Colorless to summon, the 2/2 Brothers of Fire may seem to be overly expensive. Even their ability hardly seems worth it. If 2 Red mana and 1 Colorless are spent to activate it, the Brothers deal 1 damage to a target creature or player and 1 damage to you.

The Brothers of Fire, however, can be dangerous indeed, especially when methods are available to avoid the damage which they inflict upon their controller. While a Circle of Protection: Red is usually adequate, far better to place a Spirit Link on the Brothers and gain life while using their powers. In this case, each activation of their power nets you 1 life, while dealing one damage to your opponent.

Note that this power is also one which does not require tapping, making a Spirit Linked Brothers of Fire a better investment by far than a Prodigal Sorcerer. Multiple targets can be taken out in a single turn, without exposing the Brothers to the effects of the Royal Assassin or similar nonsense. In addition, at 2/2, the Brothers are safe from the usual sort of assault leveled against creatures which possess special abilities. The Rod of Ruin and the Prodigal Sorcerer both will need assistance before they can take out the Brothers of Fire. On the other hand, the Brothers of Fire can take out creatures too powerful for the Rod or Sorcerer to kill on their own.

On the attack, the Brothers can be used to soften up a defensive line before being thrown into battle themselves. Another method of using them involves weakening a creature that they are about to block, or one which has been reduced in toughness as a result of combat.

Using Mana Flare to make their ability more affordable is one popular way of increasing their effectiveness. And even if you do not possess the ability to defend yourself against the damage they inflict, it is often more desirable to take the damage from the Brothers of Fire and at the same time take out opposing creatures.

The Brothers of Fire are not without their drawbacks. Their ability is an expensive one to utilize, and seldom will you be able to take advantage of it more than two or three times in a single turn. In addition, a single Backfire spell can turn them into little more than an expensive liability. Caution must be exercised with the Brothers, for as it is with so many Red spells, there are unpredictable consequences to their use.

Bandares assumed a smile, trying desperately not to appear unnerved. The Brothers of Fire were renowned over Torwynn for their prowess in battle and their resistance to magicks. The appearance of one on a barren rockface, on an island, was disconcerting even to the mercurial Bandares.

"Time is it, to be one or not at all."

Bandares blinked. The Brothers were also famed for their pattern of speech which made comprehension almost impossible. The Brother pounded the butt of his spear on the ground and then pointed to the rockface.

Without warning, a boulder sank into the ground, and a gout of steam erupted from the tunnel behind. The Brother entered, motioning for Bandares to follow.

Shrugging, Bandares ducked his head and entered the tunnel. Behind him, dragging the bronze box, came his assistant.

Detonate

(Antiquities, 4th Edition)

"You're certain?"

El-Hajjaj nodded, pointing to the rockface. Striations and scratches marred its surface, the source of which could not be determined. Ariana stepped up to the boulder and placed her hand on its surface. A gremlin sat atop it, watching her every move intently.

"He has been here. No more than half a day"

"Step aside. . . ."

Ariana stepped back as Canticle gathered in his will and focused on the boulder, willing it to ***Detonate****.*

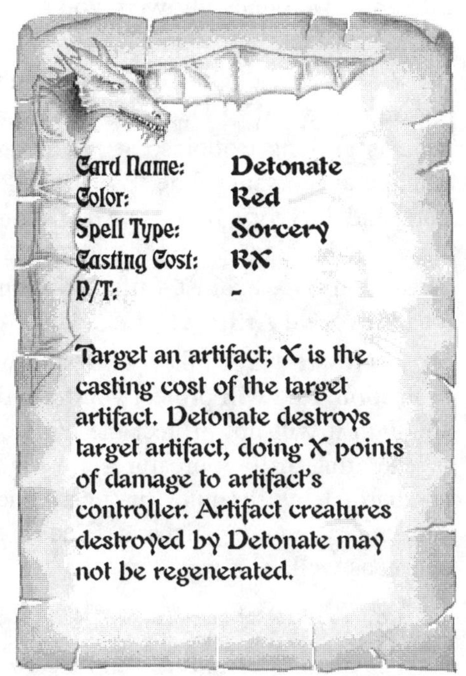

At a cost of 1 Red mana plus X, where X is the casting cost of the target artifact, Detonate destroys a target artifact. At the same time, it deals X damage to the target artifact's controller, and artifact creatures destroyed in this manner may not regenerate. This is a deadly weapon in the anti-artifact arsenal of any Mage.

It is in its ability to damage your opponent that the most obvious benefit of Detonate lies. While Shatterstorm, Disenchant and Shatter will all rid you of an artifact, none of them damage your opponent while doing so. Crumble even grants your opponent life. The only drawback to this is the cost.

Detonate is most useful against Artifact creatures, for a wide variety of reasons. Not only is it getting rid of a beast and preventing it from regenerating, it is also damaging that creature's controller. If you place a Creature Bond on the creature before detonating it, damage can effectively double as a result of the spell. In addition, you can use Ashnod's Transmogrant to create creatures for Detonation. This is definitely recommended against creatures like Drudge Skeletons or The Drowned, especially when you have no other way of coping with a regenerating creature. Ashnod's Transmogrant also expands the usefulness of Detonate, allowing you to use it even against those who do not use artifacts.

While Artifact Creatures are often the preferred target, there is no reason not to utilize Detonate against more standard fare. If a Rod of Ruin is proving troublesome, Detonate will get rid of it and deal 4 damage at the same time. Even smaller Artifacts like the Library of Leng and the Ivory Tower can be Detonated, ridding you of a nuisance and inflicting damage at the same time. Detonate is also something to consider for use against artifacts which have been stolen from you by means of Steal Artifact and Aladdin.

There are ways of avoiding the worst of Detonate. A Circle of Protection: Red will protect you from the damage caused by the spell, although it will not protect the targeted artifact. Red Wards on your regenerating artifact creatures are highly recommended, since being bombarded by shrapnel that was once your Living Wall is never amusing. Counterspells and Blue Elemental Blasts are always an option as well.

BLAM

The gremlin catapulted into the air as the perch upon which it was sitting detonated with a bang. Pebbles and dust settled to the ground, revealing a moisture-coated passage beyond. Steam wafted forth from the opening, while a wave of heat washed over the companions.

Canticle brushed dust particles off his vest, and then motioned towards the entrance.

"After you?"

Dwarven Warriors

(Alpha, Beta, Unlimited, Revised, 4th Edition)

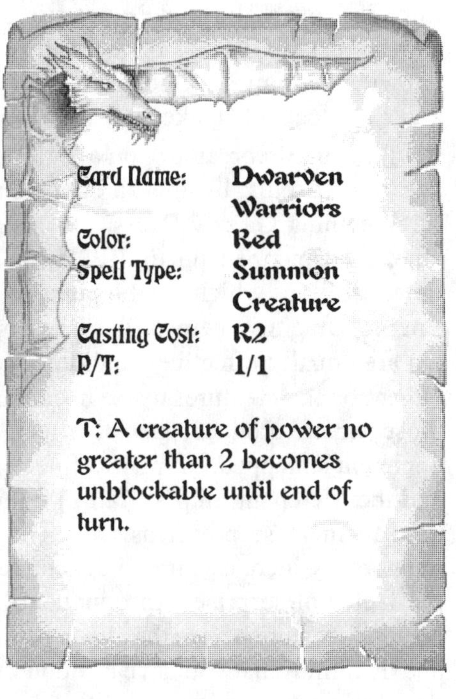

The Lord of the Mountain had had about enough. After wandering for the better part of the day through the strangely life-laden woods of the valley, he'd finally come to a pass in the mountains. His goblin scribe close behind, he had picked his way through cold water streams, brush, and fields of nettles only to find his way barred by the three men who now stood before him. Horned helmets were perched atop their wrinkled brows, beady eyes the only feature which could be seen from beneath immense, bushy beards and bulbous noses. They wore mail of intricate design and wielded axes of brilliant workmanship. All the Lord of the Mountain knew was that they were in his way.

"Look here, you stunted little nuisances, I simply don't have time for any nonsense about the safety of the valley. I want out of your valley, pure and simple. Its mere existence offends me."

In his anger and frustration, the Lord of the Mountain could be forgiven his petulance. In better times, he would have known better than to insult ***Dwarven Warriors****.*

At a cost of 1 Red and 2 Colorless mana, these 1/1 creatures are among the most versatile warriors available to a Mage. When they are tapped, a target creature with power no greater than 2 becomes unblockable until the end of the turn. However, that creature may have its power increased by other methods after it has been rendered unblockable.

In its most basic form, the ability of the Dwarven Warriors allows you to make a wide variety of 2/2 creatures unblockable, able to inflict damage upon your opponent with little to fear. Grizzly Bears, Scathe Zombies, even Hurloon Minotaurs can all attack without worrying about blockers. In and of itself, it is a useful ability, but the clause allowing the power of those creatures to increase after they have been made unblockable makes it truly potent.

Placing Firebreathing on a 2/* creature allows you to inflict damage limited only by the amount of mana that you have available. Firebreathing Grizzly Bears, for example, can be rendered unblockable, then pumped up to 10/2 with minimal effort. Creatures with innate abilities which can be pumped, like the Frozen Shade, Dragon Engine, Dragon Whelp, Killer Bees, or in the same vein, Murk Dwellers are equally effective candidates for use with Dwarven Warriors. Other popular creatures to use in conjunction with the Warriors include those which produce special effects when they get through to an opponent untapped. Hypnotic Specters, Necrites, Mindstab Thrulls, and the Merchant Ship all fall into this category. Other spells can be used to increase power as well. Giant Growth and Blood Lust can temporarily increase an unblocked creature's power and benefit from the factor of surprise. An opponent has the option to Terror an Enchanted creature before the attack begins. If he or she wastes that terror and then finds that you have a Blood Lust in hand, he or she may regret that decision.

It isn't just straight damage that can be effectively inflicted through use of the Dwarven Warriors. A large number of creatures possess abilities which are detrimental to your opponent should they get through unblocked. The poisonous nature of Pit Scorpions and Marsh Vipers, for example, or the ongoing touch of The Fallen. Naf's Asp is another creature whose power is essentially doubled should it remain unblocked.

The Dwarven Warriors themselves can be used more than once a turn as well. Simply use the Fyndhorn Brownie, Elder Druid, or Jandor's Saddlebags to untap them after they have used their power, and they can be used again.

With all of these benefits, there are obviously drawbacks. Since the ability requires tapping to use, they are highly vulnerable to the effects of Paralyze or the blade of a Royal Assassin. In addition, due to their meager toughness, a single Prodigal Sorcerer or Rod of Ruin can terminate them. Nevertheless, they are an incredibly worthwhile investment in a spellbook constructed to take them into consideration.

One of the warriors simply snorted, turning his back on the Lord of the Mountain. The other two stood their ground, giving no indication that they were about to move. Frustrated, tired, and more than just a little impatient, the Lord of the Mountain raised his hands in a gesture of surrender.

"I really haven't time for this, but since you insist on making it difficult. . .take me to your leader."

Eternal Warrior
(Legends, 4th Edition)

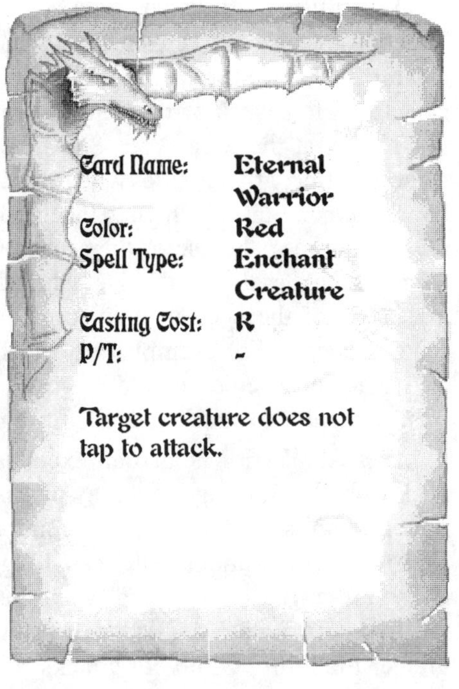

The scent of sulfur and the tang of metal filled the steam-drenched air, assailing the lungs with every breath. Hassan took the lead, Canticle close behind, neither one willing to let the other too far out of sight. Ariana did what she could to keep up, long scarf wrapped around her face. . . the conditions in the tunnel were far from ideal for someone of her constitution. El-Hajjaj brought up the rear, his hand glowing softly and providing the small band with barely adequate supplies of light. The skittering and scampering of tiny feet filled the corridor as Canticle's gremlins patrolled. The occasional squawk of protest erupted whenever one ran into a wall in the dark.

Round a corner, Hassan nearly collapsed as he brought himself to a halt. Blocking the corridor, a long sword in each hand, was a swarthy, well-muscled, yet strangely delicate young man. The Ashashid drew his own scimitars, motioning for the others to step back, for he was about to face an ***Eternal Warrior****.*

A Creature Enchantment costing 1 Red mana, this Enchantment is well worth the cost. When attacking, a creature Enchanted by Eternal Warrior does not tap.

The immediate benefits of such an ability are obvious. No longer are your attack decisions based on whether or not a creature is needed on defense, since it is now capable of providing both offensive and defensive services. Beasts which may once have been considered too valuable on the attack to hold back for defense can serve adequately in both roles, making creatures such as the Thicket Basilisk, Infernal Medusa and Abomination that much more valuable. Eternal Warrior can be even more valuable when combined with specific spell strategies, as outlined below.

When using Meekstone, you are almost invariably limited in your selection of creatures: either those which have a power less than 2, or creatures like the Serra Angel, which inherently does not tap when attacking. However, Eternal Warrior expands this selection by an order of magnitude, at the least. Your Shivan Dragon, once hobbled by Meekstone, can freely fly the skies with Eternal Warrior. This same strategy can be used when Stasis is in play. Placing Eternal Warrior on key attackers allows you to make use of them without having to worry about losing them for the duration of the duel when they tap out. It also allows you to make use of the special abilities of a creature which may otherwise require tapping. For example, the decision whether to have a Karplusan Yeti attack or whether to hold it back to destroy a creature no longer has to be made. It can attack and still make use of its ability later in the turn.

Eternal Warrior is also an excellent counter to a wide variety of spells which your opponent may put into play in an effort to slow you down. Smoke will not have an impact on creatures with Eternal Warrior. Enchantments such as Magnetic Mountain and Thelon's Curse are also circumvented when the creatures you are using never tap to begin with. In this manner, Eternal Warrior allows you far greater flexibility with your attacks.

The scream of metal against metal grated on the ears as Hassan and the warrior launched a flurry of attacks. Blades maneuvered in deadly spirals and intricate patterns faster than anyone could follow, strokes and counterstrokes falling hairsbreadths short of their targets.

It was frighteningly elegant, almost entrancing. When Hassan's opponent finally fell, victim of a cut which Canticle would forever swear had not come close to landing, silence filled the corridor. The Ashashid sheathed his blades and turned to his companions.

"We have not the time to waste. . . ."

Flashfires

(Alpha, Beta, Unlimited, Revised, 4th Edition)

The litter bearing the Queen of Cameshbaan was borne by the only surviving villagers, a pair of muscular, brawny youths who had been rescued from the charred wreckage of the inn by the scaled green Ogre which was forever at the Sorceress Lady's side. It was a completely random act of destruction on the part of the Beast. . .one moment, the villagers were waking for another day beneath black skies, and the next there was an explosion. A fountain of fire had erupted from the village well, incinerating everything in a wide arc around it. Wherever the liquid fire touched earth, it ignited timbers, scorched fields, and set ***Flashfires****.*

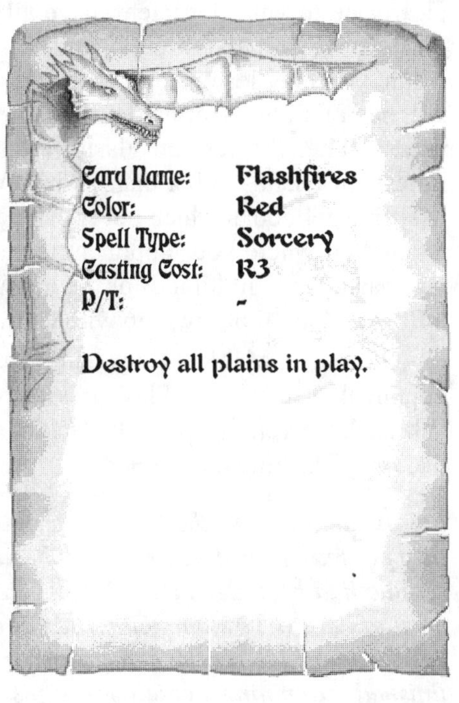

At a cost of 1 Red mana and 3 Colorless, this particular piece of sorcery does an excellent job of denying a White Mage the source of his power. Once cast, all plains in play are destroyed, making it a potent spell indeed.

Unlike Tsunami, which has a similar effect on Islands, Flashfires doesn't have to concern itself overly with being countered. White possesses very little in the way of counterspell ability. Because of this, the Red Mage can afford to wait in order to cast Flashfires.

Combined with other spells and effects, Flashfires can be truly devastating. Using Illusionary Terrain, for example, you could turn all of an opponent's Forests into Plains (assuming he or she is playing Green/White). When this is done, cast Flashfires to destroy his entire mana reserve. If your opponent is making use of a specialty land like Oasis, hit it with Phantasmal Terrain before casting Flashfires to insure that it is caught in the inferno.

With Magical Hack and Conversion, even more options are opened up. Rather than turning all Mountains into Plains, which would clearly be to your detriment, have all Swamps turned into Plains, or whatever it is that your opponent is using in conjunction with Plains. While you may lose resources as a result of Flashfire, your opponent will be out all of his or her land. Magical Hack on its own can even be used to alter the text on Flashfires, so that you can burn Swamps, Forests or Islands rather than Plains. As a result, this spell often finds itself in spellbooks which never even expect to face a White mage. In a situation where your opponent is making use of large quantities of non-basic land, multilands or the Ice Age multilands for example, use a Blood Moon. Follow it up with Conversion, and then Flashfires.

Of course, Magical Hack can be turned against you. Cast by your opponent, it can hack Flashfires to read Mountains, crippling you. White, however, is woefully lacking in anything capable of really handling Flashfires, making this an excellent sideboard spell.

Inside the litter, the Queen carefully examined one of her nails as they passed by burning fields and headed towards the mountains. Her retinue had been decimated by the unexpected disaster in the village, most of her possession incinerated along with the Inn. She had, however, managed to rescue a large number of texts and tomes, and as she finished examining herself for signs of damage, she turned to the largest one.

"This beast is going to have to learn proper etiquette."

Goblin Artisans

(Antiquities, Chronicles)

In the gorge which connected the vibrant forest valley of Yarrow with the rest of Easthold, directly beneath the hole in the sky, a tribe of goblins did their best to make sense of just what was going on. Shamans, stripped to their frayed breeches and plastered with mud and excrement, were dancing around bonfires, calling on elder spirits to explain to them what was happening. Mothers comforted their children in dank caves, assuring them that yes, someday the sun would come back.

Card Name:	**Goblin Artisans**
Color:	**Red**
Spell Type:	**Summon Creature**
Casting Cost:	**R**
P/T:	**1/1**

If desired, tap Goblin Artisans as you cast an artifact, and flip a coin. If opponent wins flip, your artifact is countered. Otherwise, draw another card from your library. You may use this ability only once for each time you cast an artifact.

In the warriors' cavern, overlooking the gorge, a different kind of ceremony was taking place. Tik-Tik, Chieftain of All, had come to a momentous decision. Obviously, the Dwarves of Yarrow had kidnapped the sun, and were plotting against the goblins. War was an inevitability, and the Goblins of Mung would draw first blood. Already, a dozen goblins were gathered around a wicker latticework, working feverishly under the direction of ***Goblin Artisans****.*

At a cost of 1 Red mana, these 1/1 creatures almost seem to be a wasted investment. Their special ability is not only limited to certain situations, but can backfire as easily as benefit. When you cast an artifact, you may tap the Goblin Artisans. A coin is then flipped, and a call made. If the call is in your favor, you may draw another card. If the call is in your opponent's favor, the artifact is countered.

First, let us examine the Artisans themselves. As Goblins, they are subject to the benefits provided by the Goblin King, Goblin Shrine and Goblin Caves, all of which combine to make them a little more appealing than other 1/1 creatures. Indeed, they can easily be used to fill out a Goblin Deck. This is a simple exercise in basic tactics. Of what use is their special ability?

The most obvious situation in which to use the Goblin Artisans is in response to a spell or effect which is countering your Artifact. At this point, you have nothing to lose on a coin toss, and the potential exists for you to draw another card, so why not take the opportunity to do so?

There are more specific situations where the Goblin Artisans may be of use as well. Using 0 cost, expendable artifacts in a reanimation deck, for example, is one way to take advantage of the Artisans. If you have an Argivian Archaeologist in play, start bringing out things like the Ornithopter, and tapping the Artisans in response. Even if they go to the graveyard, you can bring them back with the Archaeologist and try again. If you're trying to move through your library in search of specific spells, this kind of tactic may prove necessary.

If a Haunting Wind or Energy Flux is in play, a lot of your artifacts may suddenly become liabilities as opposed to benefits. Using the Goblin Artisans whenever you cast your remaining artifacts becomes a requirement, not only to try and draw additional cards, but also due to the fact that losing the coin toss isn't going to lose you the duel. If you have Grave Robbers in play, this kind of maneuver may even be highly recommended, as the more artifacts you have in the graveyard, the better. Along the same lines, if you're using low-cost artifact creatures, and also have a Lhurgoyf, the addition of creatures to the graveyard as a result of a failed coin toss is hardly a complete waste.

All in all, take care when making use of the Artisans. The perception that they are completely useless is false, but they are hardly a utilitarian force. They can serve you well, but only when properly analyzed and applied.

Tik-Tik looked with pride on what his tribe had accomplished. The wicker baskets were ready, the coals were being heated, and soon his armada would take to the skies, to drop screaming death down upon his enemies. A simpering little goblin with a lazy eye hobbled up to Tik-Tik, bearing an immense cloth patch. Tik-Tik nodded, giving him leave to speak.

"Er, ah. . .sire sir. . .where does this go?"

Goblin Balloon Brigade

(Alpha, Beta, Unlimited, Revised, 4th Edition)

The Lord of the Mountain looked up into the black sky, arms still fully outstretched. The dwarves hadn't moved in what must have been hours, and simply stood their ground, watching him carefully. He couldn't believe that they had the audacity to treat him in such a manner. His goblin scribe sat on a rock, forlornly picking at a scab on his knee.

Card Name:	**Goblin Balloon Brigade**
Color:	**Red**
Spell Type:	**Summon Creature**
Casting Cost:	**R**
P/T:	**1/1**

R: Gains flying until end of turn.

"Oi! Left says I!"

The voice appeared to emerge out of the heavens, and so startled the Dwarves that they turned their attention from the Lord of the Mountain to the source of the cry. An indistinct dot in the sky grew larger and larger, eventually resolving into the form of a wildly drifting balloon. Shouts and cries of anger emerged from the direction of the balloon. On closer inspection, one could see that a crude skull and crossbones had been painted onto the surface of the balloon. The basket suspended beneath it swayed dangerously, as the occupants began shouting.

"Ho dwarves! Prepare to be slaughtered by the omnipotent legions who crew this here vessel of the ***Goblin Balloon Brigade!****"*

At a cost of 1 Red mana, the 1/1 Goblin Balloon Brigade is a typical goblin creation. With an activation cost of 1 Red mana, the Balloon can be turned into a flying creature. This gives the Balloon Brigade certain advantages over other creatures.

At its cost, the Balloon Brigade is one of the cheaper flying creatures available to the red mage. The ability to have an active flyer by the second turn of a duel is not something to be understated, as has been demonstrated with the Scryb Sprite. In addition, since the Balloon is crewed by Goblins, it garners all the benefits and advantages due to it from the Goblin King, Goblin Caves, and Goblin Shrine. While a 1/1 Balloon crewed by goblins may inspire more laughter than fear, a 3/4 Balloon is something else entirely.

The ability to determine when to fly and when not to fly is also an advantage. A Red/Green Mage can wreak havoc using Hurricane, and then activate the Goblins when the skies are clear. When used in conjunction with Blood Lust, this tactic is devastating. First damaged by the Hurricane, then by unblocked, Blood Lusted Balloon Brigaders, an opponent is often left in a position where defeat is inevitable. The same strategy can be used with Earthquake: activate the Goblin Balloon Brigade, then cast Earthquake, saving them from destruction. While less malicious in nature than the Brigade/Hurricane strategy, it can save you from a great deal of hassle.

In addition, the activation cost can be used multiple times in a turn, even though the Goblins may only be granted Flying once. This allows you to tap lands that might otherwise damage you as a result of a Power Surge, and is a highly recommended course of action.

Properly used, the Goblin Balloon Brigade can be more than just a source of amusement. It can be a source of great irritation to your opponent as well.

The largest dwarf shook his head in amazement as he rummaged around in his satchel. This had to be a product of goblin creativity.

"Yuir lettin' us drift, fool!"

CRACK

"Not so close!"

The balloon drifted dangerously close to the edge of a cliff as the dwarves watched in baffled amazement. The largest dwarf pulled up his crossbow, carefully placing a bolt in the cocked weapon. He took careful aim at the skull painted on the balloon. As the goblins realized what was taking place below, a solitary voice echoed in the silence.

"Oh gods. . . ."

THWACK

The bolt thwacked into one side of the balloon, and exited out the other, tearing a hole in the poorly stitched fabric the size of a melon. Hot air hissed out of the balloon, and the basket rocked back and forth wildly as the goblins took to fighting amongst themselves.

"I TOLD you we should have walked. . . ."

"I gets blisters though. . . ."

Turning their attention back to the Lord of the Mountain, all trace of amusement drained from the Dwarves' faces. He was nowhere to be seen.

Goblin Shrine

(The Dark, Chronicles)

Tik-Tik knocked back the wineskin as if it were full of water, rather than cloying wine. The Balloon Brigade had failed in their mission, and it would only be a matter of time before the Dwarves retaliated. He scratched at his coat, infested as it was with lice and vermin, and sighed. Outside, the shamans continued their wild, frenetic dancing, calling upon the spirits to aid them in their time of troubles, praying before the images adorning the ***Goblin Shrine****.*

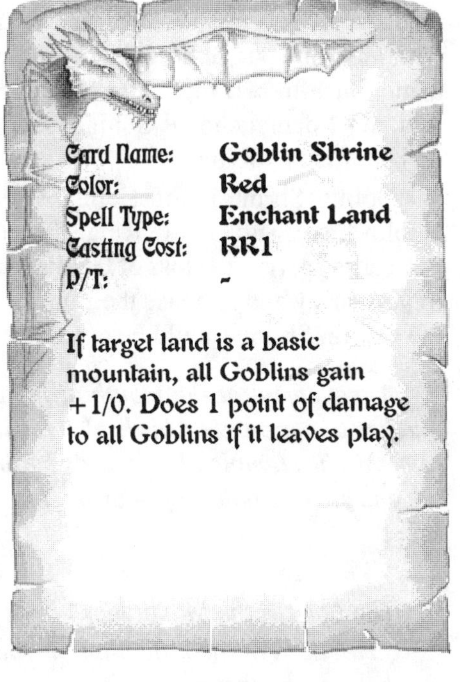

At a cost of 2 Red and 1 Colorless mana, this enchantment can be placed on any land. Only when it is placed on a mountain, however, will it provide +1/0 to all Goblins in play. However, should Goblin Shrine leave play, it will deal 1 damage to all Goblins in play.

Due to the detrimental effects which are inflicted should it leave play, a great deal of emphasis should be put on proper placement of Goblin Shrine. Ideally, it is put on a Mountain belonging to your opponent, since he or she will be loathe to destroy the Mountain in order to get rid of the Shrine. While this still leaves it open to anti-enchantment magic, it does tend to render you safe from Land Destruction. Once placed, your Goblin army acquires that much more power for use on the attack.

While the Goblin Shrine seems straightforward enough, there are other ways of making use of it. One of the more popular methods is as an anti-goblin weapon. Place it on a Mountain of your choice, use Flash Flood to return the Mountain to its owner's hand, and the Goblin Shrine is destroyed, dealing one damage to all Goblins in play. Alternately, you could simply Boomerang the Shrine into your hand, saving it for use yet again. Since its removal affects all Goblins in play, this applies to your opponent as much as it does to you. Note that Goblin Shrine does **not** have to be placed on a Mountain for this particular tactic to work. If you really want to threaten an opponent who plays with Goblins, put Goblin Shrine on your Plains to dissuade him from using Flashfires. If the Plains are destroyed, they take the Shrine with it, doing 1 damage to all Goblins. And since it is on Plains, it provides no benefits to goblins.

Goblin Shrine is most effective when used in conjunction with Goblin Caves and Goblin King. The combined benefits from the other two cards prevent the loss of Goblin Shrine from destroying large parts of your army and increase their power level as well. In a Goblin Deck, the Goblin Shrine should be considered a staple component.

A movement at the mouth of his cave caught Tik-Tik's attention, and he spun around on his heels. A brilliant light momentarily blinded him, and he stumbled backwards against the cave wall. Silhouetted in the entrance, a halo of fire around his head, was a human in brilliant robes.

"Who be ye?"

The Lord of the Mountain stepped forward, extending a hand.

"The Lord of the Mountain, at your service. Now, I do believe we can help each other out."

Ironclaw Orcs

(Alpha, Beta, Unlimited, 4th Edition)

"Things are finally beginning to look up. . . ."

The Lord of the Mountain clasped his hands behind his back and rocked to and fro on his heels, watching the preparations taking place in the gorge below. Goblins scampered about like ants who had been kicked out from their hill, performing their assigned tasks with zeal. With the arrival of the Lord of the Mountain, they seemed to believe that their savior had arrived.

The Lord's goblin scribe sat atop a large boulder, scribbling furiously as Tik-Tik's tribe broke camp. Normally, goblins were not renowned for their initiative, drive, or speed in the completion of their tasks. However, these particular goblins were being encouraged by a band of ***Ironclaw Orcs****.*

Card Name:	**Ironclaw Orcs**
Color:	**Red**
Spell Type:	**Summon Creature**
Casting Cost:	**R1**
P/T:	**2/2**

May only block creatures of power equaling 1 or less.

At first glance, these 1 Red mana, 1 Colorless 2/2 creatures seem a poor investment. While no more expensive than Grizzly Bears, the Orcs cannot be assigned to block any creature with a power greater than 1.

At a cost of 2 mana total, the Ironclaws have a decent power to mana ratio, and are a decent choice as an early attacker. Since their defensive capabilities leave much to be desired, one may as well throw them into battle in the early stages of a duel as often as possible Blocking a 1/* creature with these creatures isn't nearly as useful as dealing 2 damage to your opponent.

There are other applications for the Ironclaw Orc beyond that of mindless footsoldier. Since Ironclaw Orcs are incapable of blocking any creature with a power over 1, they are ideal creatures for use when facing Lured Basilisks, Wretched, or Infernal Medusae. While your other creatures may be falling before the scythe, the Ironclaws provide you with 2/2 creatures capable of counterattacking.

In an Orc or Goblin strategy spellbook, the Orc General can also be used to boost the abilities of the Ironclaw. With Goblin Warrens in play, there will be no shortage of sacrifices for the Orc General to use. A 3/3 Ironclaw is hardly a wasted creature. Somewhat more risky, although potentially more rewarding, is the use of the Orcish Captain with Ironclaw Orcs. While the potential exists for the Ironclaw to become 4/2, it could conceivably be killed at the same time. However, if your Ironclaws are about to be killed while attacking, you have very little to lose by activating the Orc Captain.

If you're eager to use the Ironclaws on defense, for whatever reason, spells like Weakness or Spirit Shackle, or artifacts like the Staff of Zegon can be used to lower the power of attacking creatures, allowing the Ironclaws to block. The Sorceress Queen is an ideal companion to the Ironclaw Orcs for this very reason. This can free up more powerful defenders for use elsewhere. Hardly ideal, it is something to take into consideration in desperate situations. In general, the Ironclaw Orc is an adequate footsoldier.

The Lord of the Mountain nodded his head in approval, pleased with the progress. Turning to his scribe, he rubbed his hands together in glee.

"Now, all we need is a general."

Tapping his writing quill against his chin, the goblin scribe labored in thought. Blinking rapidly, a thought occurred to him. Pointing down to the gorge below, he singled out the largest of the Ironclaws, and motioned to his master.

"Excellent choice. . . ."

Keldon Warlord

(Alpha, Beta, Unlimited, Revised, 4th Edition)

Lugash wasn't your standard orc. Standing two heads taller than his compatriots, it seemed that an equal amount of intellect had been portioned out over a larger expanse of body. His bravery, and stupidity, were legendary. No one was ever sure whether his ability to stand before a foe without quaking in fear was the result of monumental courage, or the inability to comprehend just what kind of danger he was in.

Now, his status was being rewarded. High above the gorge, the Lord of the Mountain worked elder magics, transforming the hulking Orc into a living engine of destruction. A decision had been made, and Lugash was about to become a ***Keldon Warlord****.*

Card Name:	**Keldon Warlord**
Color:	**Red**
Spell Type:	**Summon Creature**
Casting Cost:	**RR2**
P/T:	*/*

Power and toughness equal number of non-wall creatures in play on your side, including Warlord.

At a cost of 2 Red mana and 2 Colorless, the Keldon Warlord is one of the most potentially devastating creatures available to Red. The power and toughness of the Keldon Warlord are dependent on the number of non-wall creatures in play on your side, and this includes the Warlord. For example, if there are 5 creatures including the Warlord on your side, the Warlord is 5/5.

The easiest way to increase the power of the Keldon Warlord, obviously, is through the introduction of large numbers of creatures in as short a time as possible. While the usual options of low-cost, fast mana creatures are more than adequate, there exist other methods of building up the Keldon Warlord.

In a Goblin spellbook, the easiest way to rapidly increase the power of the Keldon Warlord is through the use of Goblin Warrens.

The Warlord counts only the creatures in play, regardless of whether they are actual cards, or whether they are tokens. With enough mana, 4 goblins can be turned into 6, resulting in a Keldon Warlord which is +2/+2 larger than when it had started. Given the low casting cost of goblins generally, and their color, this tactic is one of the most popular.

Other colors can prove just as worthwhile in building up the Warlord. Black has the Breeding Pit, which will guarantee an increase in the power and toughness of the Warlord each and every turn. White can use the Icatian Town to instantly increase power and toughness by 4, a nasty surprise. Green has a wide variety of methods of creating Saprolings, all of which count towards the building of a larger, more powerful Warlord. Titania's Song can create a sudden increase in the number of creatures as well, as can the activation of a Jade Statue or Mishra's Factory.

The key to effective use of the Warlord lies in hiding its actual potential in terms of buildup. An attacker may commit forces which he feels leave him with adequate defense. Use Ray of Command, however, and one of those creatures not only comes under your control, but also adds to the power of the Warlord. On the next turn, the use of Icatian Town provides a quick +4/+4 to the Keldon Warlord, a power increase which your opponent may not have been anticipating. The Homarid Spawning Bed can be used in much the same manner. Sacrificing a Homarid Warrior to the Spawning Bed creates 5 new creatures, which greatly increases the strength and ability of the Keldon Warlord.

Due to its nature, the Warlord is best destroyed almost as soon as it enters play. Terror, early Lightning Bolts, Disintegrate and Fireball are all popular methods of destroying the Warlord. Note that since the Warlord decreases in power as the creatures which build it up are slain, it is usually ideal to take out as many opposing creatures as possible before targeting the Warlord. A 5/5 Keldon can't be killed by a Lightning Bolt, but if you take out 2 Goblins with your Prodigal Sorcerers, that 5/5 Keldon is now 3/3.

Lugash doubled over in agony as the change took hold. His mail armor seemed to stretch taut over bulging, rippling muscles, while his helm cracked and splintered in a sickening manner. Antlers sprouted from beneath the ruined headpiece, sending goblins scrambling in terror from their new General.

Picking up his great axe, Lugash looked up at the Lord of the Mountain, his benefactor. With a grisly laugh, he offered him his allegiance and gratitude.

Atop the ledge, the Lord of the Mountain grunted in satisfaction.

"It's about time someone paid me some respect."

Magnetic Mountain

(Arabian Nights, Revised, 4th Edition)

Bandares continued down the passage, wiping beads of sweat from his brow, wondering where the Brother of Fire was taking him. Behind the Mage, his spindly assistant continued struggling with the bronze box from the ship, panting, tugging and pulling for all he was worth. The Brother said nothing, gave no indication where they were heading. He simply continued down the passage.

It finally dawned on Bandares just what that insistent tug on his mind was. The entire journey through the passage, a nagging sense of familiarity had been gnawing at him, and a strange noise had been on the edge of his perception. Tuned to the magicks as he was, it became clear to him that it was the mountain itself. Running a hand along the passage wall, he felt a pull on his ring. It was as he suspected—they were deep within the bowels of a ***Magnetic Mountain****.*

At 2 Red and 1 Colorless mana, this Enchantment is the bane of Blue Magi everywhere. The power of the mountain is such that, while in play, no Blue creature may untap until it has paid four mana to do so.

Though glaringly obvious, the primary function of the Mountain bears mention. Forcing a Blue Mage to spend four mana to untap a creature not only renders him or her offensively crippled, but also pulls mana away from potential counterspells. A Blue Mage who is continually forced to pay mana to untap his or her Air Elemental will not be able to cast effective Power Sinks, something which is most certainly in the best interests of those who have felt the sting of counterspells in the past. This alone makes it a frightening addition to the Red arsenal. Consider the havoc which could be wrought with Riptide. All Blue creatures are tapped, and with the Mountain in play, each one will require four mana to untap.

Not so obvious is one use which is gaining increasing popularity. It involves the placement of Magnetic Mountain in a Red/Blue spellbook. Many would consider this counterproductive, but this simply isn't the case. Using Thoughtlace on your opponent's more powerful creatures puts them at the mercy of Magnetic Mountain, while your own Blue creatures can escape the effects through Chaoslace or Alchor's Tomb. In addition, Magnetic Mountain can also be affected by Sleight of Mind. This gives you the option of using the Mountain against spellbooks which don't even make use of Blue. Sleighting it to Green, for example, can cripple a spellbook which relies on Llanowar Elves and Ley Druids to provide quick mana.

Magnetic Mountain can be devastating in conjunction with other colors as well. With Tsunami, an opposing Blue Mage may find all of his or her creatures tapped and no Islands left with which to pay the untap cost. The Necromancer can use the Royal Assassin to pick off those creatures which remain tapped. The Icy Manipulator and the Elder Druid can be used to tap creatures as well. With Magnetic Mountain, the opportunities to do harm to your opponent are boundless.

A soft red glow from the corridor head indicated that they were almost at the end of their journey. The Brother of Fire turned to face Bandares as they reached a slight incline in the tunnel.

"Far go as I am, this is. For now contest true it be. . . ."

Bandares blinked as the Brother of Fire stepped up towards the glow, disappearing from sight. Whatever was he babbling about? Snapping his fingers, he motioned for his assistant to follow. Grasping the bronze box in his weathered little hands, the assistant obeyed.

Stepping into the chamber, Bandares knew fear for the first time in his life.

Mana Clash

(The Dark, 4th Edition)

The nature of the Beast is such that chaos made tangible runs through its veins. Realities twist and collide in the air surroundings its flesh, possibilities and dreams come into being and wink out of existence before you're even aware that they exist. Perceptions are altered, ideas twisted and deformed.

Across Torwynn, the meeting of two minds caused a backlash unlike any other ever felt. In the Mourning Lands, a wretched old man cried tears of blood. Blacksand's eldritch, mysterious Magistrate fell to the ground, spiders crawling forth from open wounds. The litter bearing the Queen of Cameshbaan fell to the ground as she erupted into screams, her flesh shifting before her eyes. All victims of a ***Mana Clash****.*

Card Name: Mana Clash
Color: Red
Spell Type: Sorcery
Casting Cost: R
P/T: -

Choose a target player. You and he or she should flip a coin. Any player whose coin comes up tails loses a life. Repeat until both player's coins come up heads simultaneously.

A long-maligned sorcery, Mana Clash costs a mere 1 Red mana, and for good reason. The chaotic nature of Red is emphasized with this spell, which forces both duelists to flip coins. Each time an individual's coin comes up tails, he or she must take 1 damage from the Mana Clash. Only when both coins come up heads do the effects of this Sorcery cease to exist.

The obvious question in the mind of the neophyte is why? What possible use could there be in the casting of such a sorcery? The obvious answer lies in the proper timing and application of this spell in the right circumstances. When one utilizes the magicks of White, for example, a simple Circle of Protection: Red prevents each incident of damage from Mana Clash, while your opponent will suffer the consequences. An even better choice in white magic is Reverse Damage, cast once the Sorcery has worn itself out. Having Healing Salves, Streams of Life and Alabaster Potions in reserve after the Mana Clash has ended can also serve admirably in terms of softening the blow. In each and every one of these circumstances, Mana Clash serves to inflict a random amount of damage to an opponent (indeed, quite possibly none) while prior preparation allows you to prevent the more deleterious effects.

Of course, many still ask why. A Lightning Bolt will not bite back, and it is more certain to inflict a set amount of damage on an opponent for the same price. Mana Clash benefits from the mere threat of a randomly determined amount of damage. So long as you are willing to accept a potential loss, Mana Clash can serve you well. Indeed, in one particular duel, the opponent was so surprised at the appearance of such a random spell that he simply neglected to counter it, though he was capable of doing so. Tossing his fate to the whims of chance, he lost 5 life, and a Drain Life finished him off. Indeed, in a Black/Red spellbook, Mana Clash can be a perverse, yet strangely complimentary counterpart to Drain Life. Once the Clash has resolved, use of Drain Life not only drags your opponent down further, but also results in a restoration of life to you.

Mana Clash also has certain advantages over Lightning Bolt when used on your opponent. If your foe has a Circle of Protection: Red, Mana Clash can encourage him to tap out, as each point of damage requires a separate activation of the circle. Avoiding the damage from three or four activations of Mana Clash can be as crippling as taking the damage from one successful Lightning Bolt. Indeed, if you have a Lightning Bolt in hand, it may pay to cast Mana Clash first, in the hopes an opponent will tap out his or her land in the activation of a Circle of Protection. If the Circle isn't activated, he or she takes damage. If it is, it gives you more options to attack or cast more direct damage.

Bandares stood before the Beast, inspired and appalled. The creature sat on a throne of liquid fire, tapping ebony talons against the arm. Glacial eyes looked out over a dog's muzzle, taking in the Mage and his companion with a single, dismissive glance. For a creature known far and wide as the Beast, it was almost a disappointment.

When Bandares heard it speak, he knew then how it had acquired its name. In his lifetime, he couldn't hope to achieve the callous, chill monotone which emerged from the Beast's throat.

"Now then, Bandares. . .let a real contest begin."

Mana Flare

(Alpha, Beta, Unlimited, Revised, 4th Edition)

In the passage, all was silent. Ariana slumped against a wall, a trickle of blood dribbling out one side of her mouth. Dead or unconscious, it seemed of little consequence. The journey through the passage had been hard enough on her constitution, but the chaotic impact of the Beast proved too much. El-Hajjaj sprawled on the ground like a rag doll, babbling incoherently, alternating between paranoid visions of the Beast and memories of his childhood.

Card Name:	**Mana Flare**
Color:	**Red**
Spell Type:	**Enchantment**
Casting Cost:	**R2**
P/T:	**-**

Each land produces an extra mana of its normal type whenever it is tapped for mana.

Hassan helped Canticle to his feet and shook his head. From this point on, it would be the Ashashid and the Necromancer. Though both had staggered under the impact of the mana clash, neither had fallen. And with the eruption of magical energies, there had come a ***Mana Flare****.*

Costing 1 Red an 2 Colorless mana, this Enchantment causes an increase in the amount of mana produced by land. While in play, Mana Flare causes each land to produce an additional mana of the type it would normally provide.

Mana Flare is often used in conjunction with spells such as Fireball, Stream of Life, Howl From Beyond, Drain Life or other such spells. Anything where the power is dependent upon the amount of mana you dump into it can potentially benefit from Mana Flare. In this case, understanding your foe can allow you to benefit while he or she suffers. In those instances where I have had the opportunity to utilize Mana Flare, I followed a few simple steps which gave me the edge over my opponent.

One thing to always keep in mind is the potential for mana burn. Always make sure that you have some way of avoiding it. A Black Mage can dump excess mana into a Frozen Shade, Green has the Killer Bees, and Red can rely on the Goblin Balloon Brigade, while Mishra's Factory is an option for all. Another way to avoid mana burn is to make sure that there are least two or more spells in your hand which require large and variable amounts of mana. Drain Life and Fireball are two of the most popular, although Stream of Life and Alabaster Potion are options as well. With Mana Flare, you effectively double the power of these spells, creating the potential for a great deal of damage or a large increase in life. Using Celestial Prism to bleed off excess mana is another option to consider.

The great danger of Mana Flare is that it provides the same benefits and dangers to your opponent as it does to you. Since you are the one playing the Enchantment, though, you have the advantage of foresight. If your opponent is playing Red, it is generally a wise idea to keep Mana Flare from entering play, unless you enjoy the prospect of a 10-point Fireball on the fifth turn. If you are facing off against Blue, having a Red Elemental Blast handy to counter potentially devastating Power Sinks is something to consider. And while Mana Flare is in play, make sure that your opponent doesn't have anything in play that can funnel off excess mana. If your opponent is incapable of channeling out the large amounts of mana produced as a result of Mana Flare, add a Power Surge to the mix. Now, tapped lands are virtually a requirement, yet at the same time produce more mana than can safely be handled.

Ultimately, the best use of Mana Flare is to power your own magicks. Throwing double strength Fireballs, Drain Lifes and Streams of Life can quickly move a duel into your favor with little effort. A worthy addition to many spellbooks indeed.

Hassan drew his scimitars and nodded to Canticle, who was still brushing off his vest.

"A strange thing, fate, to bring you and I together at this time. It will not prevent me from killing you when this is done."

Canticle nodded, snapping his fingers. A soft, pale glow surrounded his hand, and he made his way up the corridor.

"One of these days, Ashashid, I will take time out to explain what happened.

Orcish Artillery

(Alpha, Beta, Unlimited, Revised, 4th Edition)

Card Name:	**Orcish Artillery**
Color:	**Red**
Spell Type:	**Summon Creature**
Casting Cost:	**RR1**
P/T:	**1/3**

T: Does 2 damage to any target and 3 damage to you. Misprint: Alpha version lists casting cost as R1.

Tik-Tik watched nervously as his goblins maneuvered the immense contraption into position under the guidance of the orcs. He wasn't sure this scheme was going to work, but the Lord of the Mountain had ordered it done. And Tik-Tik was just a simple chieftain—what did he know of the workings of magic?

The goblins scampered out of the way as the orcs began maneuvering a winch into position. Cries filled the air as four orcs were chosen at random to operate the machine and were dragged into position. Tik-Tik winced, while the Lord of the Mountain set down a strange checkered board and began placing small black-and-white statues atop the surface.

"Care for a game?" he inquired, seemingly oblivious to the operation of the ***Orcish Artillery****.*

At a casting cost of 2 Red and 1 Colorless, the 1/3 Orcish Artillery may also be tapped to deal 2 damage to a target creature or opponent. At the same time, however, it deals 3 damage to its controller.

Early in the duel, Orcish Artillery can serve well enough on its own as a blocker. By the time it is summoned, there usually isn't much out that will cause it problems. It is later in the duel, when its special ability would seem to be least worthwhile, that this construct can prove the most effective.

While it would initially seem counterproductive to utilize the Orcish Artillery as a direct damage device, meting out 2 damage while taking 3 yourself, there are numerous methods available of avoiding the damage. There is always the standard Circle of Protection: Red. For the price of activating the Circle, you can deal 2 damage to an opponent or one of his creatures. This can be particularly effective after the Artillery has blocked a creature, as the now wounded creature can be finished off by tapping the Artillery. Far more effective is the placement of Spirit Link on the Artillery. You will now be receiving a net gain of 2 life for every use of the Artillery, rather than losing three.

Even without protection from the damage, the Orcish Artillery can still prove worthwhile. If you're being slowly whittled down by the Murk Dwellers, for example, far better to use the Artillery and kill the Dwellers than take 4 damage every time they attack. The same concept holds true for any creature which may be attacking you. If it's a choice between taking 4 damage over several turns or 3 damage in one shot, it is preferable to remove the source of long-term damage as soon as possible.

As the Lord of the Mountain finished setting up the pieces to his strange game, a tremendous explosion rocked the gorge, sending bits and pieces of granite everywhere, shaking earth loose from the sides of the mountain, and causing goblins to scramble for cover. Tik-Tik looked up from beneath the log where he had sought shelter to see the Lord of the Mountain nonchalantly standing some fallen pieces back up on the board. Looking down into the gorge, the goblin chieftain saw that the artillery piece had blown a hole in the side of the mountain, which was belching forth gouts of steam.

"Now, how about that game?"

Shatterstorm

(Antiquities, Revised)

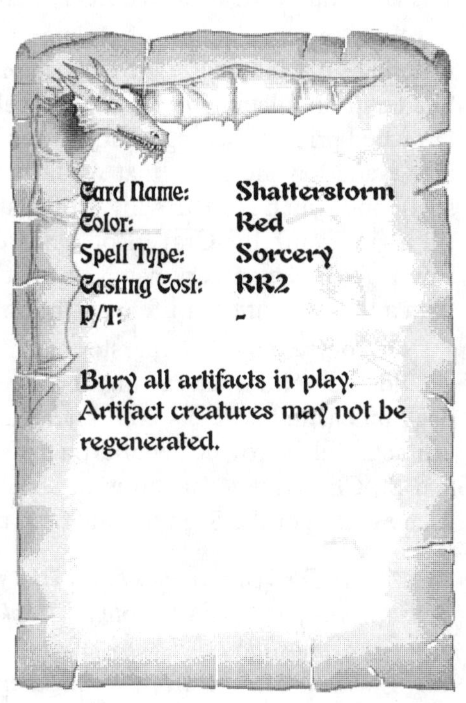

The Beast paced the length of the cavern, the dull glow of the walls casting dark, flickering shadows dancing across the area. Bandares sat mutely on the bronze chest, the limp form of his assistant sprawled before him. In a demonstration of his power, the Beast had sucked the life from the pathetic little creature.

"You still doubt my abilities, Bandares. . . ."

The blonde mage simply shrugged.

"They exceed mine. Do they exceed Canticle's?"

The glow of the cavern walls dimmed, limning everything in a sinister red aura. The Beast uttered words long unspoken in an ancient tongue. Bandares leapt from the bronze chest as he recognized the syllables. The chant was the beginning of a ***Shatterstorm****.*

At a cost of 2 Red and 2 Colorless mana, this sorcery can cripple an artificer. Once cast, all artifacts in play are buried.

The most destructive uses of this spell are fairly obvious. If your opponent is relying upon even a few artifacts to hold onto his seat of power, Shatterstorm can quickly tip the balance in your favor. The loss of two or three defending artifact creatures, a Library of Leng and Ivory Tower, or a Winter Orb and Icy Manipulator can rapidly end what may once have been a stalemate. Anecdotal evidence is all that is needed to prove the effectiveness of this spell. A colleague of mine once faced an opponent who had a Living Wall and Clay Statue acting as renewable defenders. Combined with an Ivory Tower, these artifacts were posing an almost impossible dilemma. The blockers would regenerate from every attack, while the Ivory Tower kept building up life. A quick Shatterstorm ended the impasse. Shatterstorm also affects artifact tokens, so those creatures created by the Serpent Generator and The Hive can be dealt with quickly and efficiently.

With the application of Ashnod's Transmogrant, key defenders which are not inherently artifacts can now be destroyed by means of Shatterstorm. Placing it on Drudge Skeletons, an Uthden Troll, or The Drowned prior to casting Shatterstorm can quickly destroy defenders above and beyond those that would normally be affected. Since any spellbook which is destroying artifacts en masse like this will quickly fill a graveyard, the Grave Robbers are a nice companion to Shatterstorm. After the sorcery has been cast, the Robbers can provide you with a large quantity of life over the course of the next few turns.

Of course, since Shatterstorm affects your artifacts as well, one should be careful when casting. It is often a wise decision to either hold back on casting artifacts until after Shatterstorm is cast, or use those artifacts which provide benefits on their destruction, such as the Onulet and Su-Chi. Another tactic is to sacrifice your artifacts to creatures such as Atog or the Sage of Lat-Nam, and then utilize Shatterstorm.

Across Torwynn, ancient magicks shattered before the fury of the Beast. In the Artificer's temple in Blacksand, the Copper Tablet fell to dust. In Cameshbaan, the tower of the Vizier simply ceased to exist, taking with it centuries of art and artifice. In Barze, far to the west, Ravensguard rocked on its foundations, threatening to fall off its perch.

And in a chamber beneath Easthold, Bandares was bombarded with fragments of bronze and iron, the box he had recovered from the deep exploding from within. He looked up at the Beast with derision.

"I went through a great deal of trouble to recover that . . . ."

Bandares may have been able to threaten and bully those lesser than him with his attitude, his nihilistic disregard for life and consequences. The Beast simply shrugged.

"You'll be going through a great deal more."

Smoke

(Alpha, Beta, Unlimited, Revised, 4th Edition)

Goblins and orcs poured through the opening in the side of the mountain, weapons at the ready, thirsting for blood and vengeance against their ancient enemy, the Dwarves of Yarrow. The Lord of the Mountain stood by the scorched entrance to the cavern, dictating to his scribe while Tik-Tik watched the entire event from the top of a boulder.

At the head of the column, beneath the mountain, the Orcish scouts stopped, trying to get their bearings. The explosions which had opened this passage had also created a large volume of mystical ***Smoke****.*

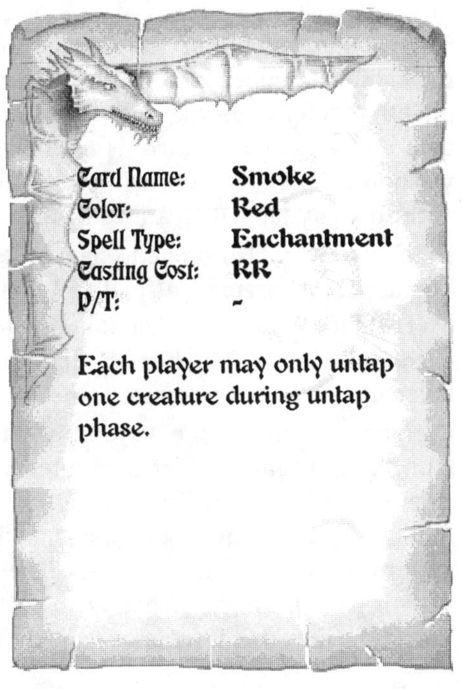

At 2 Red mana, this Enchantment is an extremely potent weapon. While in play, it prevents participants in a duel from untapping more than one creature during their untap phase

Smoke is best utilized when the casting Mage has the means to untap his or her creatures through a variety of methods after the untap phase. Use of Jandor's Saddlebags, Eternal Warrior, or creatures which do not tap while attacking, or Twiddle are some of the more common methods of bypassing Smoke. The Windseeker Centaur is a popular choice of creature, since it is the same color as the Enchantment. In a multicolored spellbook, Norrit can be used to help untap Blue creatures. Johan, if available, is the ideal creature for use in conjunction with Smoke.

This enchantment can be particularly deadly when teamed up with spells which either force your opponent to attack or which tap his creatures. Riptide can be used to force all blue creatures to tap, or with the use of Sleight of Mind can be used to force any single color of creature to tap. Icy Manipulator, Twiddle, and the Elder Druid can force creatures to tap as well. One particularly effective use of Smoke involves casting Siren's Call, followed by Fog, Darkness, or some other magic which prevents damage from an attack. With all of his or her creatures tapped, your opponent will be hard-pressed to mount an effective defense during your turn, and will be unable to untap more than one so long as Smoke is in effect. A Royal Assassin is an ideal weapon in this situation, while a Nettling Imp will have a field day with so many tapped creatures to choose from.

Smoke can also prove to be a brutal reinforcement of the overall "untappable" strategy, a spellbook which revolves around the use of Meekstone, Winter Orb, Damping Field, and Smoke. Yotian Soldiers, Serra Angels and Windseeker Centaurs are the primary creatures in this concept deck, for obvious reasons.

There are also some ways in which Smoke can be used to devastating effect against objects and items one might not otherwise consider. For example, if Kormus Bell is in play, the untapping aspect of Smoke applies—now your opponent will be unable to untap his or her swamps for mana. This same method can also apply to Titania's Song. Not only is the Song preventing an artifact from using its abilities, but Smoke insures that it remains tapped as well.

The orcs and goblins milled about in confusion for a few moments before the hazy cloud of mystical energies cleared enough for them to continue. The oppressive heat and humidity remained, however, and they were reluctant to move on. Behind them, the shouted admonishments of Tik-Tik, backed by the presence of the Lord of the Mountain, convinced them that retreat was not an option. Ahead, the cavern took on an angry red glow. . . .

Stone Giant

(Alpha, Beta, Unlimited, Revised, 4th Edition)

The Queen of Camesh-baan was not amused. Hands at her hips, a glare in her eyes, she tapped her foot impatiently as her litter bearers continued the repairs to her preferred mode of transport. She tugged on the leash in her hand, and her ogre companion returned to her side, back from the side of the road where he had been rooting amongst the bushes.

While the mana clash had caused her a moment of pure terror, as her flesh shifted and flowed before her eyes, it had quickly returned to normal. Her litter bearers, however, were not so fortunate. Her scream had attracted the attention of a nearby ***Stone Giant****.*

Card Name:	**Stone Giant**
Color:	**Red**
Spell Type:	**Summon Creature**
Casting Cost:	**RR2**
P/T:	**3/4**

T: Give one of your creatures with toughness less than Stone Giant's power flying until end of turn. Target creature, which can increase it's toughness after it gains flying ability, is killed at end of turn.

At 2 Red mana and 2 Colorless to summon, the Stone Giant is a 3/4 collection of solid muscle. Not only is it a power in its own right, but when tapped, the Stone Giant can hurl a creature through the air, granting it the ability to fly until the end of the turn. The unfortunate creature is killed at the end of the turn, however, when it lands. The only stipulation is that the creature cannot have a power greater than that of the Stone Giant, and the creature must be under your control.

By far one of the most popular methods of using the Stone Giant's powers is in conjunction with creatures which provide some sort of benefit on their demise. The Rukh Egg, when imbued with Giant Growth or Blood Lust, becomes a deadly flying missile which also provides a 4/4 flyer on its death. Blazing Effigy can function in much the same manner, while the Onulet is another option for tossing. Note that the creature granted flying only needs to have a power less than the Stone Giant at the point when the ability is granted. After that, placing a Howl from Beyond or Blood Lust is not a problem.

If an opponent is lacking in flying defenses, more interesting uses can be devised. One particular mage is fond of creating venomous serpents with the Serpent Generator, and imbuing them with flying. Using regenerating creatures as missiles for the Stone Giant can be equally irritating. Having Uthden Trolls repeatedly thrown at one's head does not do much for the ego. This particular method of using the Stone Giant allows for defensive implementation. Using the Serpent Generator or a Master of the Hunt to provide fodder for the Giant every turn gives you an effective flying screen. The Breeding Pit can also be used to provide expendable aerial defense as well. Ideally, you can steal your opponent's creatures by means of the Old Man of the Sea, Preacher or Seasinger, and use them as ammunition.

Stone Giant can be particularly brutal when teamed with Jandor's Saddlebags, the Elder Druid or the Fyndhorn Brownie. With these in play, the Giant can grant flying to several creatures in a turn, or can grant a creature flying and join in the attack. Alternately, it could also be used on the defensive.

The Giant now sat in the middle of the road, watching the small creatures which had entered its territory with interest. When it first arrived, it had mistaken them for intruders, and had hurled one of them into the next valley. Their panicked reactions, and the foul curses which had erupted from the box two of them had dropped piqued its curiousity. Now it was looking upon them with a different eye.

The Queen noticed this interest, and her irritation began to subside. She sauntered up to the Giant, a gleam in her eye.

"Great one. . .perhaps you could be of assistance to one who is new to this land. . . ."

Wheel of Fortune

(Alpha, Beta, Unlimited, Revised)

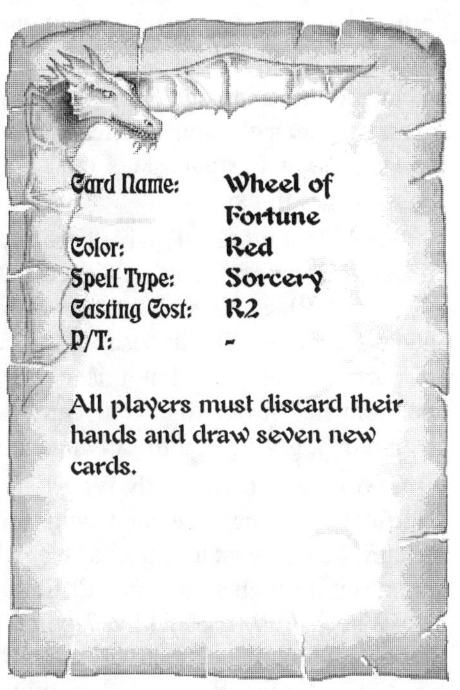

Canticle and Hassan entered the chamber fully expecting to find Bandares in wait for them. The sight of the Beast, however, was something else entirely. Beneath his aura, Bandares appeared pathetic and childish, a pale reflection of the evil that he represented. Among the Ashashid, there is a saying that evil pales before apathy, for it is still driven by emotion. In this chamber, that saying seemed to take on life.

The Beast smiled at their entrance and pointed to the far wall.

"The contest begins, Canticle. . .not what you expected, I'm sure, but after our last little dance, I decided on a new selection of music."

The wall faded and drained away as if it were mist, revealing a strange, elaborately carved ***Wheel of Fortune****.*

At a cost of 1 Red and 2 Colorless, this Sorcery is a work of chaotic deviousness. When cast, all players discard their hands, and draw seven new cards.

This spell has practical applications across the spectrum, both offensive and defensive. While one could spend volumes discussing the intricacies, the more powerful and easily available combinations will be concentrated on.

The best situation in which to use this spell is when your own hand is depleted or non-existent, and your opponent has a wealth of cards available. Any plans he or she may have had will be ruined, while you attain a whole new hand at a relatively low cost. To make things worse for your opponent, use a Braingeyser to fill his or her hand with more cards than he or she could conceivably use, and then cast Wheel of Fortune, forcing him or her to discard them all. If your opponent has just used Diabolic Vision, Brainstorm, or similar magics, Wheel of Fortune is also recommended, as it will foul their carefully laid plans. All of this while you simply may be attempting to fill your hand.

Diabolic Vision and Brainstorm can also be to your benefit. After casting these spells, put the least valuable card into your hand, then cast Wheel of Fortune. This cuts out chaff, leaving you with your chosen cards in hand.

In an even more offensive capacity, Wheel of Fortune can be used on an opponent after you've placed a Black Vise or two in play. While a first-turn Black Vise always deals damage, you aren't always guaranteed a first-turn Black Vise. In the later stages of the duel, you may have several in play, but this doesn't do you much good if your opponent has fewer than four cards in hand. Wheel of Fortune can change this, giving you the advantage in the situation.

The classic tactic with Wheel of Fortune is its use in a library destruction strategy. Teamed with Braingeyser, Millstone, Hypnotic Specter, Mind Twist and similar magicks, Wheel of Fortune can allow you to run through an opponent's library at lightning speed. Following up a Wheel of Fortune with a 7-point Mind Twist is a classic piece of strategy, which can effectively force the discard of 14 cards in ideal situations. A properly constructed library destruction strategy, making full use of Wheel of Fortune, can prevent an opponent from ever casting a spell before running out of cards.

Obviously, there are drawbacks. There is no guarantee that you won't be assisting your foe by casting Wheel of Fortune. In at least one situation, a lackluster, weak hand was discarded and replaced with a much superior one, while the caster of Wheel of Fortune ended up with next to nothing. Such are the vagaries of chance, however. More often than not, when properly applied, Wheel of Fortune turns the tables.

Slowly, the wheel began to turn, the strange markings on its surface glowing with an unearthly light. Bandares turned to Canticle with a smile, and the Necromancer looked over to Hassan. The Ashashid was in no position to assist him—some foul enchantment had taken hold of him, and he was unconscious on the cavern floor.

"Shall you take your turn, or shall I?"

White Spells

Conversion

(Alpha, Beta, Unlimited, Revised, 4th Edition)

Stone Giant leading the way, his tree trunk limbs dragging great furrows in the soft dirt of the trail, the Queen of Cameshbaan's procession continued towards the mountains. As she watched the progress of the troupe from her litter, the Queen grew more and more impatient. No matter how long they travelled, no matter how much ground they managed to cover, they still seemed to no closer to finishing their journey than when they had started.

Suddenly, it dawned on the Queen. The eldritch magicks loose on the world were having unpredictable effects, to be sure, but the more power the Beast accumulated, the more chaotic the effects. Now, the very land itself was undergoing a ***Conversion****.*

Card Name:	**Conversion**
Color:	**White**
Spell Type:	**Enchantment**
Casting Cost:	**WW2**
P/T:	-

All mountains are considered basic plains. Pay WW during upkeep or discard Conversion.

The bane of the Red Mage, this Enchantment costs 2 White and 2 Colorless mana to bring into play. 2 White mana must be paid during upkeep or it is destroyed, but the benefits it provides are more than worth it. While in play, all mountains are considered basic plains.

When played at its most basic level, to turn all of an opponent's Mountains into plains, this spell is powerful enough. Conversion virtually eliminates the fear of Fireballs, Lightning Bolts and similar appalling foolishness, and unless your opponent is using White as well, he or she may find himself crippled for the rest of the duel. Note that since Conversion converts all mountains into Plains, it can have a disturbing effect on Multilands. Since multilands are considered lands of both types, any which contain a Mountain aspect are immediately turned into basic plains. Combining Blood Moon with Conversion can be even worse. All specialty lands are turned into Mountains, and as a result of Conversion, become Plains. Why all the converting? A one-word answer will suffice. Flashfires. If you want to take out specialty lands, use Phantasmal Terrain. Or if you want to turn his or her other lands into plains as well, rendering him helpless, use Illusionary Terrain. The possibilities are numerous.

When combined with Magical Hack, Conversion becomes even more versatile. Now, any land type can be converted into the land type of your choice, making Conversion useful against any color of deck. Swamps can be turned into plains for maximum benefit from Flashfires. Mountains can be turned into Swamps to provide added power to the Angry Mob. There are numerous ways to take advantage of this combination.

Avoiding the effects of Conversion are somewhat more problematic. Unless one has access to Disenchants or Counterspells, chances are it will enter play uncontested. Once in play, it can be crippling. The Sunglasses of Urza are almost a requirement when you expect to be dealing with Conversion, as they can counteract the effects quite nicely. Magical Hack works quite nicely as well, and multiple Hacks can turn Conversion to your benefit. In one situation, two Magical Hacks were used against a White Mage's Conversion, causing it to turn all Plains into Swamps, at which point his Bog Wraiths finished off the hapless Plainswalker.

Tugging on the leash she held in her hand, she ordered her ogre to stop. When the scaled green beast lurched to a halt, the litter bearers followed suit, gently setting their burden down. The Queen of Cameshbaan stepped out in a huff, stamping a foot against the ground.

"I will not stand for this kind of treatment. Hesenti!"

D'Avenant Archer

(Legends, Chronicles)

Those tuned to magic, or born of it, are far more sensitive to its impact than those who are products of nature. The twisted orcs and goblins are as vulnerable to the perils of uncontrolled mana as the highest Mage.

*So it was that Hesenti stepped forth. Born of humble family in Cameshbaan, he had served his life in the armies of his homeland. His skills and talents had brought him to the attention of the Queen, and since that time, he had served her as a personal bodyguard, her **D'Avenant Archer**.*

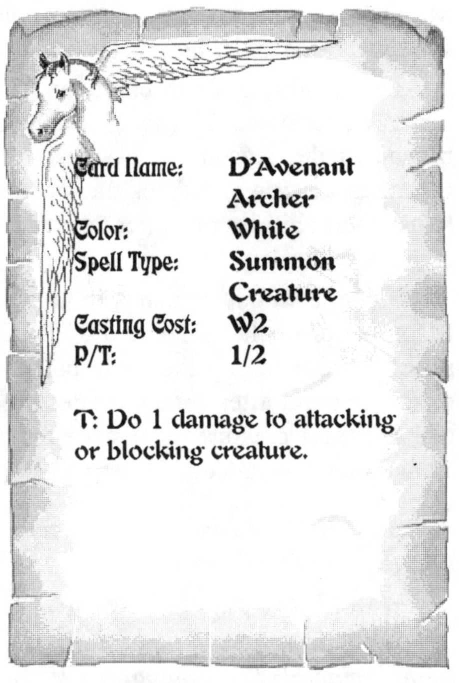

At a cost of 1 White mana and 2 Colorless, the D'Avenant Archer is a 1/2 creature which can deal 1 damage to a target attacking or blocking creature when tapped.

While it appears a simple, straightforward enough creature to begin with, the D'Avenant Archer is a formidable force to deal with. The nature of its ability makes it useful in a wide variety of situations, as well as rendering it a nuisance almost on the level of a Prodigal Sorcerer. Due to its relatively low power rating and reasonable toughness, it is best held back on defense. It is its special ability, however, that truly makes it stand out.

On the attack, the D'Avenant Archer effectively raises the power of any chosen attacking creature by one. In order to insure the survival of blockers, your opponent will have to make sure that anything he assigns to defense has a toughness at least 2 greater than the power of the creature it will be facing. Otherwise, the D'Avenant can add its arrows to the battle, killing the defender. On defense, the D'Avenant can prove just as useful. Any attacker will have to think twice before committing itself to battle. Two Hurloon Minotaurs could be facing each other in combat, and with the added bonus of the D'Avenant Archers, the Minotaur under your control would emerge victorious. Multiple Archers only add to the problems faced by your opponent in deciding when and where to attack.

The lethality of the Archers can be increased even more by forcing creatures to attack by means of the Nettling Imp, Norrit, or on a broader scale, Season of the Witch and Siren's Call. Calling over */1 creatures allows you to pick them off before they have an opportunity to use their abilities or inflict damage, a nasty but effective method of creature control.

Using methods which can untap a creature, such as the Icy Manipulator or the Elder Druid, the D'Avenant Archer can even be utilized twice during the same battle. Alternately, you can use it to attack, untap it after defense is declared, and then tap it to inflict one damage on a creature. The wide-ranging versatility of this creature cannot be understated.

Hesenti bowed before his queen, trying desperately to hide the quiver in his voice.

"I live to serve, noble one."

The Queen tapped him on the cheek, and smiled. Turning to the ogre, she nodded approvingly.

"He's so sweet. . .it's one of the reasons I've never had him killed".

Turning back to Hesenti, she pointed in the direction of the mountain.

"Now, it's simple really. You know Hassan, and you know what it is he faces. Kill them both, and you can come back. Otherwise, don't bother."

Hesenti bowed deeply, stiff with a combination of fear, anger and resentment. It was an oath he had sworn long ago, however, and one which he would not break.

"I live to serve, my queen."

Divine Offering

(Legends, Chronicles)

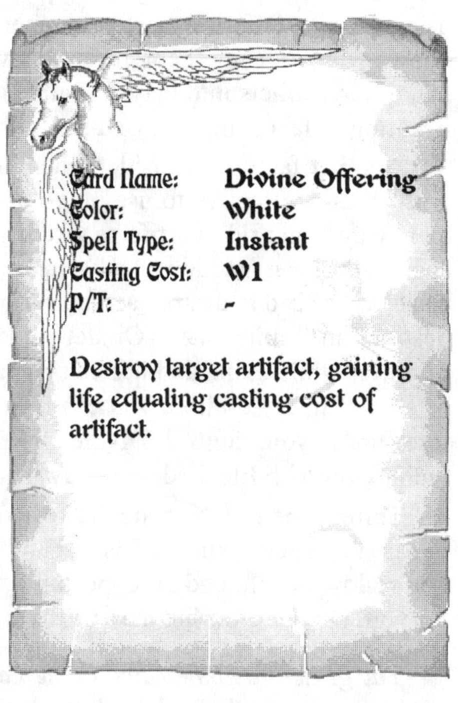

Canticle watched the turning of the wheel with vaguely concealed disgust, while Bandares rubbed his hands together with delight. The Beast simply watched, observing their reactions. The chaotic entity was gambling with the fate of an entire world, and the only thing which seemed to vaguely interest him was how the two contestants were reacting.

The Lord of the Mountain looked up from where he was sitting, examining the chamber closely. There was nothing, nothing at all, that he could use. Sighing, he reached into the folds of his robes and pulled forth a pair of wire-rimmed glasses. With an expression of pure regret, he held them in hand and mumbled a few phrases, making of them a ***Divine Offering***.

A 1 White mana, 1 Colorless instant, Divine Offering destroys a target artifact. That isn't all it does, however. The caster of Divine Offering then gains life points equal to the casting cost of the artifact.

At its most basic level, Divine Offering is an extremely efficient way of destroying enemy artifacts. Unlike Crumble, which provides your opponent with life on the artifact's demise, Divine Offering provides you with life. Whether the target is a Colossus of Sardia or a Black Vise, Divine Offering will get rid of it and benefit you at the same time.

The key to using Divine Offering to full effect is to save your Disenchants for low-cost yet irritating artifacts, while blasting away at the high-cost material with Divine Offering. While the temptation to use Divine Offering on an opposing Ivory Tower may be great, far better to wait for a Disenchant and save Divine Offering for a Jayemdae Tome. The larger and more expensive an opposing artifact, the more benefit to you from your opponent. There is an added bonus to using Divine Offering in this manner as well. Once your opponent knows you are using them, he or she will be extremely hesitant to put his or her artifacts into play. Crumble and Disenchant aren't nearly as irritating to face, since they simply destroy the artifact.

Another factor to consider when using Divine Offering is when it will be most effective to use on your own Artifacts. This spell is the ideal way to get rid of artifacts which are no longer serving a purpose, such as the Armageddon Clock. On a secondary level, Divine Offering can also be used to destroy artifacts of yours which provide benefits on destruction. Taking out an Onulet with Divine Offering nets you a total of 4 life, while mana and life can be garnered through the destruction of a Su-Chi. In addition, you can use it on regenerating artifact creatures under your control. Divine Offering simply destroys them, providing you with life, and they may then be regenerated freely.

Timing and targeting are the key components to determining when to cast this spell. When a Disenchant will suffice, use it. However, if you're low on life and an opposing artifact is making things difficult for you, Divine Offering may be the way to go.

The glasses disintegrated in the Lord of the Mountain's hand, and energies coursed through his body. While upset at the loss of a favored artifact, it had provided him with the resources he would need to fight the battle ahead. It was clear that none of the participants in this little game were willing to play by the rules, so he would just have to start writing his own.

Death Ward

(Alpha, Beta, Unlimited, Revised, 4th Edition, Ice Age)

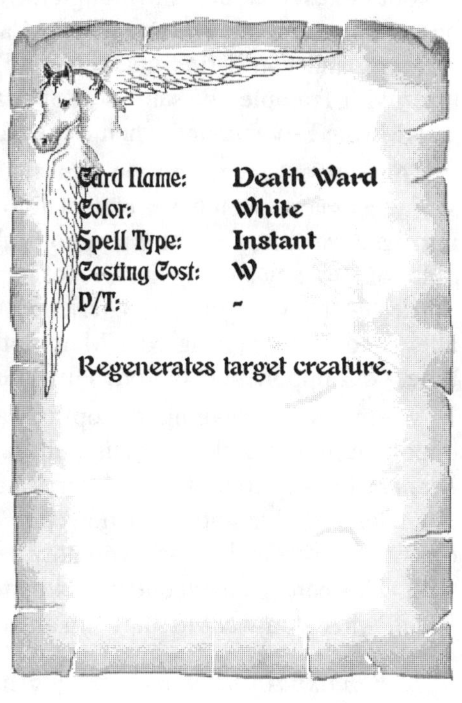

Ariana supported herself against the wall, coughing heavily into her scarf, spatters of blood marring its surface. She simply didn't have the strength, the constitution to continue. Her entire life had been a struggle against her own body, her drive and purpose the only thing keeping her alive. Deep within the earth, in the lair of the Beast, it was no longer enough.

*Canticle's eyes flickered briefly as he sensed Ariana's peril. Linked as he was to her, he knew all too well how hard the journey had been on her. His attention stolen from the still turning wheel, he channeled what energies he could spare into a **Death Ward**.*

At a cost of 1 White mana, this simple Instant provides a wealth of uses. When cast, a target creature is regenerated.

Though the ability to Regenerate on an ongoing basis would be far more useful in the long term, the nature of Death Ward makes it a worthwhile instant in times of combat. One should also take it into consideration in a straight White or a Blue/White spellbook, which is woefully deficient in regenerating creatures.

One of the best qualities of this spell is its surprise nature. Unless an opponent is making use of the Glasses of Urza, Portent, or the Orcish Spy, chances are he or she will not be able to plan an attack taking Death Ward into consideration. This gives you several options when the time comes to plan an attack of your own.

There are many occasions during the duel where a stalemate is reached, where no one is willing to commit to the attack as there are simply too many blockers to deal with. In such situations, the elimination of a single key creature can bring about a quick resolution. Send in your largest creature, and though it will no doubt be slain, it will take one or more defenders down with it. Cast Death Ward to recover your creature, and you'll find yourself with the advantage. Used on creatures with Trample, the same sort of strategy holds true. Attack, cast a Howl From Beyond, and when it dies, Death Ward it.

A one-shot Regeneration can also be useful when it comes to saving a creature you never expected to lose. Nothing is more frustrating than watching a War Mammoth about to trample your foe into oblivion, then watching it face off against Giant Growthed Scryb Sprites. A truly agonizing experience, part of the humiliation can be alleviated by recovering your Mammoths with Death Ward. Only this time, your opponent is out one Giant Growth.

Defensively speaking, the options available are just as useful. An opponent may launch a final assault, feeling that overwhelming numbers are the key to securing victory. After all, if you slaughter all the defenders, you've got an open avenue of attack. Cast Death Ward on one of those defenders, and you now have something to counterattack with. This can be an excellent backup to Siren's Call or Season of the Witch when you want to maintain an advantage in terms of numbers.

Ariana spasmed momentarily, grasping the wall in an effort to maintain her balance. After a few moments of vertigo, she recovered enough to continue on her way. In time, perhaps, she would resent Canticle for what he had done, but there was still far too much to be done.

And in order to finish things, she had to live.

Eye for an Eye

(Arabian Nights, Revised, 4th Edition)

Slowly, the wheel came to a stop, the skeletal finger which served as an indicator coming to rest on an ancient Dwarven rune symbolizing Ruin. Bandares winked at Canticle and approached the wheel to take a spin.

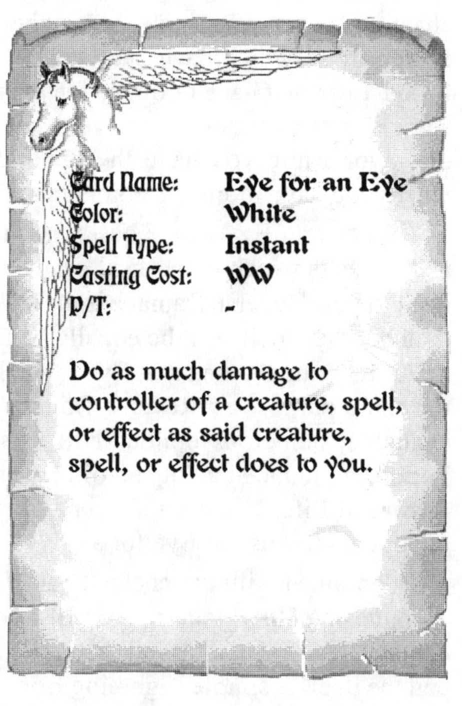

"Ooh, rough luck, old bean. One more on the dark side for me, and it's show-time."

Canticle scowled as the Beast watched their competition. It was such a ridiculous way to decide the fate of Torwynn, and yet he had little choice. Without the components, the spell which would seal the Beast in the tomb from which he had escaped would not work. And without Ariana, there were no components.

The Beast suddenly turned, launching an impossibly large bolt of energy at a form which was approaching him from behind. The bolt struck the Lord of the Mountain square in the chest, hurling him against the far wall of the chamber. The Lord of the Mountain crumbled, but still managed to shake his head as he spoke.

"Hardly sporting, but as the saying goes, it's an ***Eye for an Eye****. . . ."*

Costing 2 White mana, Eye for an Eye is an act of vengeance. An instant, it deals damage to your opponent equal to the amount of damage done to you by a creature, spell, or effect.

It is rather apparent that Eye for an Eye has its greatest utility against those spellbooks designed for what is known as direct damage. Fireballs, Disintegrates and Lightning Bolts can all be turned against their wielders with horrendous effect. Indeed, more than one practitioner of Red has met his or her end after casting a destructive Fireball, only to have Eye for an Eye create a draw.

Against creatures, Eye for an Eye is best used against those enchanted beasts who have been given tremendous, but temporary power, those which have been endowed with a Howl From Beyond, Blood Lust or Giant Growth, for example. The damage from these sources is usually a one-time event, and it makes perfect sense to return the favor while you have the opportunity, especially in a situation where you have more life points than your opponent.

Eye for an Eye works best when used in conjunction with spells and artifacts which either heal or reverse the damage which has been dealt to you. Reverse Damage is the classic followup to Eye for an Eye, though other spells can be equally beneficial. If you allow a Colossus of Sardia through, then cast Eye for an Eye. Reverse Polarity can serve the same purpose as Reverse Damage. If neither of these spells are available, numerous options still exist. Healing Salve or Alabaster Potion can reduce the impact of the damage you've received, as can a Stream of Life. In each and every situation, you're gaining over your opponent after use of Eye for an Eye.

Combined with the enchantment Justice, Eye for an Eye can give an opposing Red mage ulcers. If he or she is willing to absorb the damage dealt by Justice and casts a Fireball at you, Eye for an Eye can end the duel. A simple Lightning Bolt will deal 3 damage to you while inflicting 6 on the caster should Justice and Eye for an Eye come into play.

The Lord of the Mountain raised his arm, and a bolt of energy course forth, slamming into the Beast with enough force to knock it off balance. The creature staggered into the wall, knocking loose several boulders, which shattered as they struck it on the head

"Serves him right! Imagine striking an official. . . ."

Fortified Area

(Legends, 4th Edition)

Bandares blinked as the Lord of the Mountain launched his assault on the Beast, smug confidence draining from his features. Suddenly, things weren't looking so positive. Stepping back from the wheel, he pulled a bag of salt from his belt, uttering a series of sharp, guttural syllables. The Beast ignored Bandares and Canticle both, concentrating on the Lord of the Mountain, who was casually brushing dust and debris from his robes.

"Mountain lord, you almost amuse me. . . ."

The Beast launched a flurry of fiery missiles, which exploded in a gaudy display of pyrotechnics. When the smoke had cleared, there was no sign of the Lord. An alarmingly bizarre collection of swords, brambles, brush and shrubbery had erected themselves between the Beast and the Lord of the Mountain, encircling him in a ***Fortified Area****.*

Card Name:	**Fortified Area**
Color:	**White**
Spell Type:	**Enchantment**
Casting Cost:	**WW1**
P/T:	-

Give all your walls +1/+0 and banding.

At first glance, this 2 White, 1 Colorless Enchantment seems to be of limited value. While it is in play, all walls gain +1/0 and Banding. While obviously useful in a spellbook laden with Walls, its applications seem to be in question. Nothing, however, could be further from the truth.

The value of Fortified Area is obvious in any spellbook which puts an emphasis on the defensive capabilities of walls. Not only does it provide a small measure of offensive power, but the ability to Band extends the usefulness of many different walls. While a Wall of Wood on its own is hardly a threat, a 1/3 Wall of Wood banding with a

Krovikan Vampire is something else entirely. However, there is far more to the Enchantment than this.

Consider the combination of Fortified Area and Animate Wall. While a Wall of Swords is effective in and of itself, an Animated Wall of Swords with the ability to band and increased power becomes an actual danger to your foe. This can be a cheap and effective way to provide additional attackers—given the low-cost, high-toughness nature of Walls, they make the ideal banding attackers. For example, a Wall of Stone has one of the best toughness ratings around, yet it costs as much as a Hurloon Minotaur. Banding an attacking Wall of Stone with almost any creature can protect you from almost any blocking threat.

Animate Wall isn't even necessary in some circumstances. Consider the Walking Wall. All things considered, you could easily have a 4/5 banding attacker by the fifth turn of play, a situation that an opponent will have a hard time dealing with. Snow Fortress is another Wall which is particularly useful with Fortified Area, due to its adjustable toughness. For example, assume you are under attack by a Scaled Wurm. Banding the Snow Fortress with Balduvian Bears, you can spend an additional 3 mana to kill the Wurm. In addition to that, 3 more mana will save both your wall and the Bears from destruction. In addition, consider the Wall of Wonder, or the newly discovered Dark Maze. Any Wall which possesses the ability to attack immediately becomes a threat with Fortified Area in play.

While vulnerable to a wide array of anti-enchantment Magic, Fortified Area is protected by its poor reputation. Other more immediately threatening enchantments are often targetted instead of the Area. Keeping the above tactics in mind, Fortified Area can serve you well.

The Beast snorted in disgust, irritated more than angered by the Lord of the Mountain's escape from destruction. There would be time enough to finish him off later. He turned his attention back to the two "contestants" without even giving the wall surrounding the Lord a second glance.

Bandares turned to wink at Canticle before throwing the bag of salt into the air. His form wavered and grew transparent, his words seeming to arrive from a great distance as he spoke.

"It's been fun. . .play nicely while I'm gone. . . ."

Guardian Angel

(Alpha, Beta, Unlimited, Revised)

The Beast crossed its immense arms, drumming its fingers against knotted muscles, looking down on the Necromancer.

"It seems that Bandares has forfeited his turn. . .my spin."

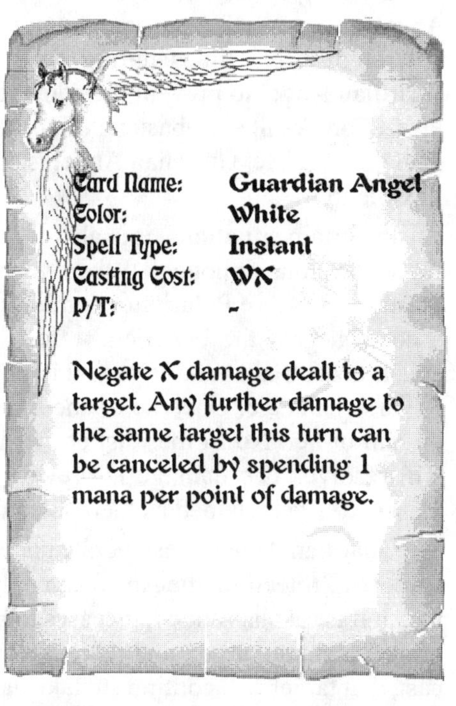

The Beast moved over towards the Wheel, placing a finger on the edge. With a flick, he sent the wheel spinning at an incredible speed, the figures and runes on its surface blurring together in a dizzying kaleidoscope of color. Canticle drew back against the wall of the cavern, wracking his mind for some sort of solution. If the Wheel stopped on one of the dark runes, Torwynn would become the domain of the Beast. And if it were a light rune, the Beast would simply spin again. . .and again. . .and again. Lacking any other recourse, he called upon a ***Guardian Angel****.*

Costing 1 White and X Colorless to cast, Guardian Angel can prevent X damage to a target from a variety of sources during a turn. As long as one has mana to expend, one can prevent damage to a target.

While Guardian Angel is often maligned, its ability to prevent damage more than once in a turn is often overlooked. Consider the situation where an opponent uses Pestilence a number of times during his or her turn. An intelligent mage spreads out the use of Pestilence for maximum effect. One 3-point Pestilence may destroy a Hill Giant, but not if you have Healing Salve. Three 1-point Pestilences over a period of time, however, will negate the effectiveness of Healing Salve in this particular situation. However, Guardian Angel can be used to prevent this damage as it takes place.

There are more uses for Guardian Angel as well. The same tactic that worked on your opponent's Pestilence can work equally well on yourself, especially in a Black/White spellbook. Using Guardian Angel on yourself, you can start pumping mana into Pestilence at several different times during your turn. Each time, you can use Guardian Angel to prevent the damage, at the same cost as a Circle of Protection. While Alabaster Potion could conceivably be used to regain this lost life, Guardian Angel is cheaper to put into play and more flexible in use.

In certain situations, it is also to your advantage to play Guardian Angel on your opponent. When your foe is making use of Reverse Damage, Reverse Polarity or similar magicks, Guardian Angel can be used to negate the beneficial effects. Damage is assessed after the attack takes place, and it is at this point that your opponent will use Reverse Damage. Once he or she has done this, cast Guardian Angel on him or her. No further fast effects take place, and Guardian Angel will resolve. The damage is prevented, and Reverse Damage takes place. No life is gained as there is no damage to reverse.

Guardian Angel does operate under limitations, however. Unlike a Circle of Protection, the Angel can only be used once. After the turn in which it is cast has ended, it ceases to be of use. In addition, it can only protect a single target, and there is no guarantee that after it has been cast, that target will continue to take damage. If a Lightning Bolt to you is prevented using Guardian Angel, an opponent can simply shift his or her next Lightning Bolt to one of your creatures. It does possess the advantage of surprise, which is something that cannot be underestimated.

Canticle completed his call and turned his attention back to the wheel. With Hassan unconscious and Ariana missing, there was nothing he could do to stop what was about to take place.

In the corridor, Ariana pulled a piece of blood-soaked cloth from her satchel. Clearing her throat, blocking out the pain, she began to chant.

Karma

(Alpha, Beta, Unlimited, Revised, 4th Edition)

*Canticle stumbled and fell against the cavern wall as the enchantment took hold, tears of blood streaming down his face. On the surface, the Queen of Cameshbaan let out an ear-piercing wail. For all the pain it caused them, however, Ariana's enchantment had the largest impact on the Beast. Its hands flew to its head, and it let loose an animal bellow of pain. Pounding its temples with its fists, the Beast tried to shake off the effects of **Karma**.*

Card Name:	**Karma**
Color:	**White**
Spell Type:	**Enchantment**
Casting Cost:	**WW2**
P/T:	-

Do 1 point of damage to a player for each swamp he or she has in play during his or her upkeep.

At 2 White and 2 Colorless to cast, this Enchantment has often proven to be the downfall of those who practice Black magick. During each player's upkeep, Karma deals 1 damage to that player for each Swamp he or she controls.

Obvious uses aside, Karma can be a potent weapon in some surprising situations. For example, few people consider the use of Karma in a spellbook which makes use of Black itself. However, through the use of Elves of Deep Shadow, Barbed Sextants, appropriate dual lands from Ice Age, or tri lands from Homelands, Black mana can be acquired without the use of Swamps. Since none of these lands qualifies as a Swamp, they are safe for use in a Karma spellbook. The surprise factor of facing off against Karma in a deck composed largely of Black can secure a victory against many Necromancers. Care must be taken, however; the original dual lands, from Bayou to Badlands, do count as basic lands based on the mana they supply and therefore can be affected by Karma. Alternately, in a White/Black spellbook, a Circle of Protection: White can be used to protect you from the more deleterious effects of the Enchantment.

In a White/Blue spellbook, Magical Hack can be used on Karma to allow its use against almost anyone. An opponent who is playing Red/Green will seldom worry about Karma, until you Hack it to read Mountain. This allows you to make use of a devastating Enchantment in a wide variety of situations, rather than limiting its use to one color.

Even if you don't possess Magical Hack, Karma can be used against a wide variety of spellbooks. Use the Cyclopean Tomb to convert large quantities of lands into Swamps. Illusionary Terrain can be used to accomplish the same goal, while Phantasmal Terrain can be used to lesser effect. Anything which allows you to convert opposing lands into Swamps, no matter how short the duration, will mean damage at the hands of Karma.

There are, however, dangers to using this enchantment. Just as Magical Hack can be used to your benefit, it can also be used against you with deadly results. Having Karma Magical Hacked to read Plains can turn the tables in rapid fashion.

The Beast fell to its knees, the source of its power tainted by the touch of Karma. Ariana staggered into the cavern, a bloodied piece of cloth wrapped around her hand, and nodded to Canticle. The Necromancer clenched his teeth, fighting back against karma's backlash, and returned the nod. It was time to begin the ritual.

Land Tax
(Legends, 4th Edition)

The Queen of Cameshbaan stumbled out of her litter, spears of pain stabbing at her eyes. Delicate, tapering fingers dug into the earth as she attempted to release her ties to the powers which were slowly destroying her. The litter bearers stepped forward to aid their mistress but found themselves warded off by the tree trunk limb of the Stone Giant.

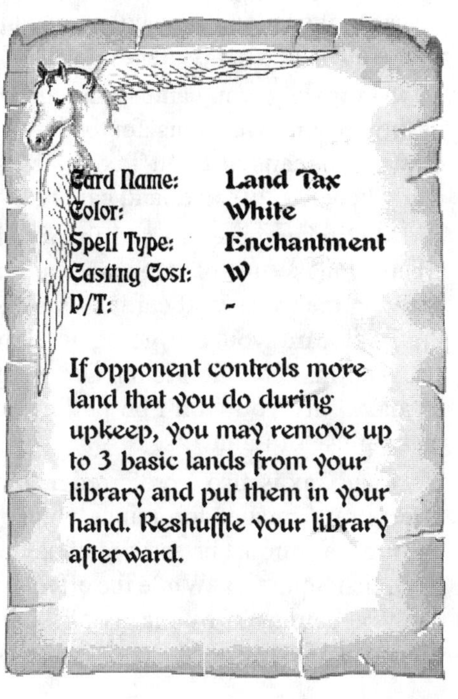

*Realizing that the source of her torment was the very source of her power, the Queen severed her connections to those lands. Bereft of power, and with confrontation imminent, she sought to replenish her powers by means of a **Land Tax**.*

At a cost of 1 White mana, this Enchantment can solve one of the most insidious problems faced by Magi: mana starvation. While in play, Land Tax allows you to search through your library for three land cards, which you may then put in your hand. This takes effect during your upkeep, and only if your opponent controls more land than you.

The immediate benefits of this spell are obvious. In numerous situations, one often finds that the resources needed to cast a spell simply aren't available, and all the while your opponent grows in power. Land Tax allows you to even the odds, pulling select land cards from your library into your hand. While this is simple and straightforward, there are various ways of making full use of this spell.

Rainbow Vale is one method of making sure that during your upkeep, you have fewer lands than your opponent. Tap the Vale for mana at any point during your opponent's turn, and it will revert to his or her control at the end of that turn. In situations where land resources are even, this tilts the balance in favor of your opponent during your upkeep, allowing you to make use of Land Tax. This not only gives you access to the lands you need, but it can also fill your hand in situations where a Black Vise is in play.

Alternately, you can use Zuran Orb or Dark Heart of the Wood to destroy your own lands for benefit, replacing them with the lands drawn by means of Land Tax, a simple tactic which can yield a great many benefits, life and land cards of your choice.

Maximizing use of Land Tax also involves making sure you know when to make use of it. Since you have to shuffle your library after drawing the three land cards, it makes little sense to use Land Tax if the next card you are going to draw will be the land you need. Brainstorm, Diabolic Vision, Orcish Spy or Visions should all be used to make sure you won't be putting yourself at a disadvantage when making use of Land Tax.

Land Tax is also a preferred method of pulling out from under the effects of Armageddon (since your opponent, for one turn after the casting, can almost be assured of having more land than you), Conquer or Orcish Squatters. While the effects of Conquer and Orcish Squatters can't be countered by means of Land Tax, the general impact of the effects can be lessened.

The Queen of Cameshbaan sat next to her litter, legs crossed in a meditative stance, arms folded over her chest. Slowly, inexorably, she gathered together the resources she felt she would need for the coming confrontation. Whoever was confronting the Beast possessed magicks capable of affecting Magi across Easthold. And anyone with that kind of power could be used.

Petra Sphinx

(Legends, Chronicles)

Hesenti kept an arrow nocked as he carefully made his way down the corridor. The broken bodies of goblins and orcs were strewn throughout the corridor, tossed aside as if they were dolls caught in the midst of a child's tantrum. A dim light flickered ahead, and the archer drew in a breath.

Suddenly, the light disappeared, plunging the corridor into darkness. Hesenti stepped back, expecting the worst, and a girlish giggle echoed off the walls. Faint footfalls sounded, and a leonine form padded into sight. Milky white wings were folded on a feline back, and most startling of all, a feminine face looked out from behind a silky mane. Hesenti blinked, dropping his arrow in surprise at the sight of a ***Petra Sphinx****.*

Card Name:	**Petra Sphinx**
Color:	**White**
Spell Type:	**Summon Creature**
Casting Cost:	**WWW2**
P/T:	3/4

T: Make target player name a card and then turn over the top card in his or her library. If the opponent's guess matches the card, it is put into his or her hand; otherwise, it goes to the graveyard.

At a cost of 3 White mana and 2 Colorless, the 3/4 Sphinx may seem to be far more expensive than it is worth. However, when tapped, the Petra Sphinx's power is activated. A target player names a card and then turns over the top card of his or her library. If the card which is turned over is the one which the player named, it is put into his or her hand. Otherwise, it is placed in the graveyard.

Since this power may be activated at any time, a popular use for the Sphinx is as a blocker, which then uses its power when its defensive capabilities have been utilized. At 3/4, it has little to worry about from many of the smaller creatures, which allows you to use it in this dual capacity without too much concern for its safety. Alternately, you can use Instill Energy, the Fyndhorn Brownie, or the Elder Druid to untap the Sphinx, providing you with multiple uses in a turn.

There are two primary schools of thought concerning how best to utilize the Sphinx. There are those who feel it should be used on opponents only, while others who feel it can be equally useful when used on yourself. Both strategies have merit.

Against an opponent, Petra Sphinx can be an excellent way to burn through an opponent's library, especially when combined with artifacts like the Millstone and the Vexing Arcanix. A Black/White spellbook can add Hymn to Tourach, Mind Twist and similar discard spells for effect. There is always a risk that the opponent will correctly name the card and place it into his or her hand, however, which makes backup artifacts or spells like Mind Warp or the Disrupting Scepter good ideas. Alternately, you can use spells or creatures such as Orcish Spy, Visions, or Portent to look at your opponent's library to determine whether something useful would be gained.

Some of the most practical applications with Petra Sphinx are when it is used to provide you with additional cards. A wide variety of spells and artifacts exist which allow you to make safe use of its ability. Diabolic Vision, Brainstorm, Orcish Spy, Visions, Field of Dreams, and even Portent can all be used to reveal the next few spells in your library. When these cards are known, Petra Sphinx allows you access to an additional card each and every turn. With the addition of Instill Energy, or through the use of Jandor's Saddlebags, you could draw 2 additional cards a turn. This kind of access to spells is an advantage that cannot be dismissed.

There are situations where a Petra Sphinx may not be nearly as useful as one might have envisioned. If an opponent is using the same sort of library-searching spells as you are, particularly Orcish Spy, Petra Sphinx is of little use against him or her. And unless you are planning on using it on yourself, there are far better creatures to have in play for the cost. In order to minimize this danger, the Sphinx is best used in a spellbook which plans on making use of it against both opponents and its controller.

Hesenti pulled another arrow from his quiver and pulled back on his bow. The sphinx tilted her head at the archer, her smile revealing a row of glistening fangs.

"And why, says I, should you seek to kill this one, when at odds we are not. The Beast is friend to you and I, I do not think. . . ."

Hesenti blinked, astonished at the presence of this creature, doubly so that it was here on apparently friendly terms.

"This is true, noble beast, but I am forced to wonder at your presence."

The sphinx laughed, an amazingly childlike sound from such a creature.

"A favor owed, one could say. . . ."

Piety

(Arabian Nights, 4th Edition)

Hassan looked up from the rubble-strewn floor of the chamber, shaking his head to clear away the stars and sparks which filled his vision. The Beast had broken its hold on the Ashashid, the spells and enchantments besieging it causing it to lose concentration. Scimitars cleared their sheathes with blinding speed and in moments were weaving a bloody pattern on the Beast's hide. Free from the constraints of the black magicks which had held him in place, Hassan drove himself with strength drawn from ***Piety****.*

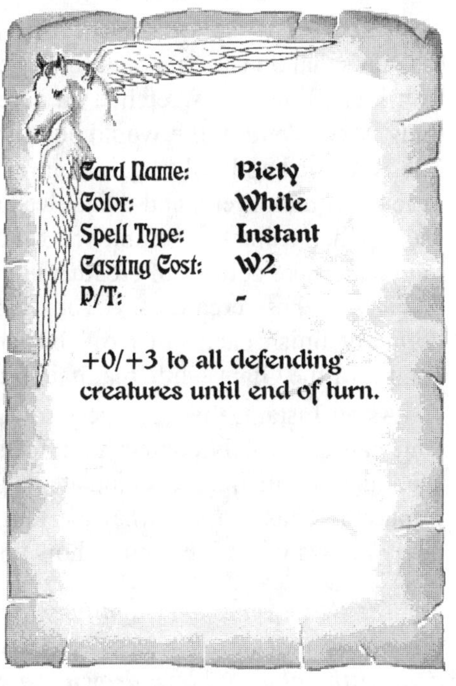

Costing 1 White and 2 Colorless, this Instant provides all defending creatures with 0/+3 until the end of the turn.

Quite apart from the quick boost this spell can give a defensive line, there are other uses which may not be immediately obvious to the neophyte. The key to successful use lies in casting Piety at the most opportune moments. For example, after casting Siren's Call and forcing your opponent to attack with all of his forces, Piety can allow your defensive line to survive the assault while inflicting heavy casualties at the same time. Combined with the effects of Castle or Crusade, Piety can be a devastating surprise to spring on your opponent. This tactic can prove to be useful in conjunction with Season of the Witch, or even Total War, although it isn't quite as effective as Siren's Call.

Another tactic available to White with this particular spell is its use in maximizing the effect of the Veteran Bodyguard, the Kjeldoran Royal Guard or the Martyrs of Korlis. Allowing large creatures to pass through unblocked allows you to concentrate your defense on other creatures, while casting Piety effectively allows you to redirect that damage to the Bodyguards without killing them. In a situation like this, the Kjeldoran Royal Guard could safely take on 7 damage dealt to you by an unblocked creature, thanks to Piety.

Since Piety isn't color-specific, it can prove devastating with creatures that one might not normally consider compatible with White. Consider using The Wretched on defense. Normally, blocking something which could kill it would be counterproductive, since you'd lose The Wretched and fail to gain control of another creature as compensation. A quick Piety, and the tables have turned. This can also prove useful when using the Seraph or Krovikan Vampire on defense, allowing you to take control of creatures which might otherwise escape the clutches of these creatures. A Tor Giant and Krovikan Vampire would normally finish each other off, but adding Piety allows you to take control of the Giant while maintaining the Vampire.

As an Instant, there are very few drawbacks to using Piety. Only Blue can effectively counter its effects, and the surprise nature of the spell makes it difficult to calculate its potential effects. When Castle is in play, it's easy to see what the toughness of a creature is, but one never knows when Piety may show up.

The Beast bellowed magnificently, spinning around to knock aside the mortal that dared wield a blade against its form. Hassan easily dodged the clumsy blow, drawing a scimitar across a tendon in the process.

"The bigger they are, foul one. . . ."

Eyes narrowing, the Beast raised a massive hand to cast a spell. The words died on its lips as an arrow smacked into its palm, pinning its hand against the wheel which was behind it. The wheel stopped, skeletal indicator resting on the Rune of Growth.

Canticle, Ariana and Hassan all turned in surprise. In the mouth of a tunnel, Hesenti nocked another arrow, while a leonine form padded into the chamber.

Repentant Blacksmith

(Arabian Nights, Chronicles)

The eyes of the Beast widened in surprise as it pulled the arrow from its palm, and that shock registered in its voice.

"How. . .?"

Ariana, still clutching at the walls of the cavern for support, approached the immense form of the Beast, a wry smile on her bloodstained lips.

"The blood of a martyr to bind your magicks, the touch of a pious man's blade, and the son of a ***Repentant Blacksmith.****"*

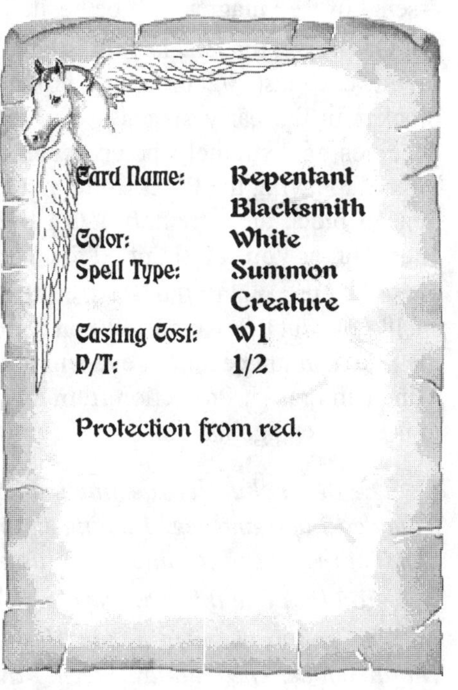

At a cost of 1 White mana and 1 Colorless, the 1/2 Repentant Blacksmith is a worthwhile investment. With Protection from Red, this creature can serve you well in a wide range of situations.

Taking into consideration the casting cost, the Blacksmith is far more useful to a White mage than something like a Pearled Unicorn, especially against one who uses Red magicks. Not only is it cheaper to bring into play, it possesses a special ability in addition to an equivalent toughness. Protection from Red insures that Lightning Bolt and similar direct damage spells will have no effect on the creature, protecting it from most of the usual anti-creature spellcraft.

When facing a Mountain Mage, the Blacksmith is best used on the attack. Goblins, Kobolds, and Orcs alike will part before the Blacksmith, allowing you clear access to your foe. Though one damage may seem to be a paltry sum, the usual Red methods of stopping an attacker will be useless. Adding Army of Allah and Crusade will insure that on the attack, the Blacksmith can deal a large amount of damage early in the duel. For its casting cost, the Blacksmith is one of the cheapest Protection from Red creatures available to White. Add to this the Enchantment of Venom, and even those who add other colors to their arsenal of Red magick will be hesitant to block it.

Of course, the Blacksmith is equally useful on the defensive. One of the cheapest */2 creatures around, it can serve as an excellent blocker in the early stages of the duel. Add Castle or Piety, and it becomes an extremely potent defender, one which need not fear a Fireball. Having the Blacksmith band with the Benalish Hero or Pikemen to block an extremely large Red creature is also a worthwhile endeavor, as you can shunt all the damage over to the Blacksmith.

All of this makes the Blacksmith a worthwhile addition to a White spellbook, but that isn't all. When combined with the Magicks of Blue, the Blacksmith becomes even more versatile. A simple Sleight of Mind can grant it Protection from any color you choose, allowing you to use it even against those who do not make use of Red.

The Beast chuckled, despite the ichor which was dripping from its wounded hand and leg. Placing its back against the wall, putting a hand on the wheel, it smiled a rictus grin.

"You lack one thing, worms. One of my own. . . ."

The sphinx sauntered into the room, an innocent smile on its childlike face. The creature's form wavered and shifted, growing black and indistinct. Slowly, the sphinx morphed, taking on the shapely form of a young woman, skin of alabaster, robes melting into the shadows. Hassan nearly dropped his scimitars while Hesenti merely gasped. There, in the center of the chamber, stood the Queen of Cameshbaan. She opened her mouth to speak, but before she could utter a word, a plaintive voice was heard from behind the wall of shrubbery and brambles which sat in the chamber.

"Is it over yet? Does someone want to let me out of here?"

Reverse Damage

(Alpha, Beta, Unlimited, Revised, 4th Edition)

A huge bolt of lightning arced across the room, smashing into the greenery with the force of a thousand arrows. Sparks and tinder flew throughout the chamber, settling to the ground in the aftermath of the explosion, the stench of ozone heavy in the air. The Beast turned to face Canticle, who was preparing a spell, and snarled in outrage.

"That pompous fop was just the first, Necromancer. . . ."

A tap on its leg distracted it for only a moment, but that was all that was needed. The Lord of the Mountain stood there, smiling, saved from a spectacular end through the effects of ***Reverse Damage****.*

Card Name:	**Reverse Damage**
Color:	**White**
Spell Type:	**Instant**
Casting Cost:	**WW1**
P/T:	**-**

All damage you have taken from any one source is added to, not subtracted from, your life total.

This instant costs 2 White mana and 1 Colorless and can prove to be endlessly beneficial. When cast, all damage taken from any one source is added to the caster's life total instead of subtracted from it.

The possibilities inherit in such a spell are boundless, and to examine all of them would take pages. Setting aside some of the more obvious uses in the area of combat, to prevent damage from creatures like the Shivan Dragon or the Leviathan, there are a multitude of combinations available which make full use of this spell.

Some of the more devastating methods of using Reverse Damage involve the use of spells one may not immediately consider. Take, for example, Drain Life. Using Drain Life on yourself is hardly what one might consider a good idea. However, with Reverse Damage, it becomes extremely beneficial. Cast Drain Life on yourself for a large amount of damage, somewhere in the area of 10 (for the sake of example). This total is the added to your life points, for a net gain of nothing. However, cast Reverse Damage, and that 10 points of damage is removed, replaced with 10 life. Now, your net gain in life is 20.

Reverse Damage can also serve well in situations where you are casting large, area effect spells which deal damage to everyone. Hurricane and Earthquake, for example, can blanket the area with a huge amount of damage. With Reverse Damage, however, you can put yourself ahead by as much as your opponent will be behind. Time Bomb is another example of how Reverse Damage can come into play. Simply activate Time Bomb, and then follow it up with Reverse Damage. To a lesser extent, this will also work with Armageddon Clock.

Another example of how Reverse Damage can prove to be useful is in combination with Blood of the Martyr. Blood of the Martyr redirects all damage from creatures to you, and if that damage arrives from a single source, Reverse Damage can turn it all into life. Pestilence can be turned into a productive source of life, and at the same time your creatures will be saved from destruction. Sorrow's Path, once thought absolutely useless, can become a source of power to you. Simply use Blood of the Martyr in these situations, and then cast Reverse Damage.

Care and caution must be exercised. There is no guarantee that your opponent won't find some way to counter Reverse Damage, and if you've expended a large amount of life hoping to benefit from its effects, you may quickly find yourself on the losing end.

"NO!"

A simultaneous barrage of magical energy slammed into the Beast from three different sides. As the creature staggered, attempting to regain its balance, an arrow sank itself into its thigh. Cursing in a tongue long forgotten, the Beast gestured, encompassing the entire chamber.

"If I fall, know that I shall take you all with me. . . ."

The ichor dripping from its wounds began to take on a life all its own, pulsing and glowing hideously. As its energies failed, the Beast channeled the remainder of its power into destroying itself.

Visions
(Legends, 4th Edition)

Beneath slate grey skies, the stagnant waters of the Mourning Lands continued to trickle by stands of lonely reeds. Somewhere in the distance, a plaintive wail was heard, and the marsh goblins hurried to appease their god. Amidst the bracken and the decay, a solitary tower stands, home to the Necromancer Emeritus.

Inside his chamber, he sits before the fire, thinking of all that he has seen. In his dreams, it is as if it were reality, though he knows it cannot be. The Beast is dead, taken from Torwynn by the hands of his oldest friend. Bandares is a memory, faded and distant, though ever present. And Ariana. . . .

Sighing, he stands, wondering at the purpose of these ***Visions****.*

Card Name:	**Visions**
Color:	**White**
Spell Type:	**Sorcery**
Casting Cost:	**W**
P/T:	**-**

Look at the top 5 cards of any library, then reshuffle it if you so choose.

Costing 1 White mana, this Sorcery allows you to look at the top 5 cards of any library. At this point, you may choose to shuffle that Library or keep it intact.

Obviously, Visions provides one with a quick method of discerning an opponent's capabilities and quite possibly fouling those capabilities by rearranging those spells. If your opponent makes frequent use of Diabolic Vision, Brainstorm or similar magics, this can be a powerful countermeasure. The potential of knowing what your opponent will be drawing can be astounding. Counterspells can be saved for the most opportune moment, destructive cards can be hoarded for creatures which may eventually appear, and elements of an opponent's strategy can be determined. One particularly nasty use for Visions involves Millstone, as you can simply wait until enough cards have been drawn to make the most efficient use of the discards. In addition, since your opponent does not share the knowledge granted by Visions, you will have the advantage of knowing what to prepare for.

Visions becomes even more deadly in concert with the legendary Nebuchadnezzar. Knowing what cards your foe will be drawing allows you to force a discard each and every time, given enough mana to properly use his ability. Indeed, anything which allows you to force a discard from your opponent gains even more utility with Visions, whether it be Vexing Arcanix or the Petra Sphinx.

Few Magi, however, realize the value of using Visions on their own spellbook. When one is in a desperate need for mana, Visions can provide you with the foresight you need. If immediate relief is not forthcoming, one can shuffle in the hopes of acquiring a better draw. Combined with the Petra Sphinx or Vexing Arcanix, this can work as well for you as it can work against your opponent.

A gremlin scampered out of the Necromancer's way as he made his way to the door of his chamber. Sparing a brief glance at the painting above the mantle, he sighed. There was so much to learn, so much to see, and so very little time. The price of knowledge, he said to himself, is seldom what one believes it to be.

Index